Service with a
SMILE

52 Humorous Sketches for Sunday Worship

DANIEL WRAY

MERIWETHER PUBLISHING LTD.
Colorado Springs, Colorado

Meriwether Publishing Ltd., Publisher
PO Box 7710
Colorado Springs, CO 80933-7710

Editor: Rhonda Wray
Cover design: Janice Melvin

© Copyright MCMXCVIII Meriwether Publishing Ltd.
Printed in the United States of America
First Edition

All Scripture quotations, unless otherwise indicated, are taken from the HOLY BIBLE, NEW INTERNATIONAL VERSION®. Copyright © 1973, 1978, 1984 by International Bible Society. Used by permission of Zondervan Publishing House. All rights reserved.

Scripture quotations marked (TM) are from *The Message*. Copyright © 1993. Used by permission of NavPress Publishing Group.

Scripture quotations marked (KJV) are from the King James Version.

Library of Congress Cataloging-in-Publication Data

Wray, Daniel, 1962-
    Service with a smile : 52 humorous sketches for Sunday worship / Daniel Wray. -- 1st ed.
      p.   cm.
    Includes indexes
      ISBN 1-56608-043-6 (pbk.)
    1. Drama in public worship. 2. Christian drama, American. I. Title.
BV289.W73 1998
246'.72--dc21   98-27080
                                                      CIP

3   4   5   04   05   06

Dedicated to my beautiful wife and children,
who never stop laughing at me.

Contents

Introduction

Sitting on a mountainside in Galilee, the multitudes listened to Jesus speak. He spoke on such things as anger, lust, revenge, and the law. And they listened. Why? They did not know at that time that he was the Son of God. Yet he kept them enraptured for hours upon hours, enthralling thousands at a time without a sound system, props, costumes, or eloquently written sermons. He kept them spellbound by the stories he told, using parables to keep their attention and creating mental imagery to make the teachings stay in their memories. It is by Jesus' example of teaching that drama is used in worship services today. "How would Jesus teach this today?" is a question I ask before undertaking any sketch. Hopefully these sketches will reflect that pursuit.

The first time we performed a sketch in the worship service of the church I attend, there was much anxiety on my part. Certainly we had done other dramatic presentations for the congregation before; in my years of working with the youth, we had put on numerous Christmas plays and a dinner theater or two. But our church, like many small churches, holds tradition in the highest regard, and change is often met with much skepticism. That's why, after doing three or four sketches during Sunday morning worship services, I was surprised at the vote of popularity they received on a congregational questionnaire. It proved one thing to me: People love to be taught in a variety of ways, and if one of those ways involves making them laugh, they often remember the message a bit better. That's the reason behind *Service with a Smile* — to give congregations of any size a worship resource that can be implemented in minutes with results that can last a lifetime.

It's been said that it's impossible to smile on the outside without feeling better on the inside. There are very few things that feel better than laughter — unless, of course, you are making someone else laugh. And if you can make them think in the process, you have really accomplished something. These sketches are designed to do just that. Growing up as a "P.K." (Pastor's Kid), I did a lot of laughing and a lot of making people laugh — but not in church. In fact, church wasn't really a very happy place to be. Yet I noticed that the members of the congregation remembered the humorous anecdotes in my father's sermons — often

1

more vividly than they remembered the context of the sermon.

Over the years, as I found my place of service in my own congregation, I discovered that entertaining people with words and actions was one of my gifts — one that felt really good to share. For the past 10 years I have served in various capacities at my church; most of these activities have involved the youth. As a high school teacher, I am aware that kids today are faced with some tough challenges and need more encouragement than ever to become involved in their church. Traditionally, this has not been achieved very effectively. I found drama to be one avenue for kids to become involved in the church service and to feel like they are a part of the church community. Since that time, the sketches included in this collection have utilized all generations on-stage to illustrate the topic of the messages delivered from the pulpit and to stimulate post-service discussion regarding the themes outlined. If you are involved in using drama in your worship services already, you know how effective this tool can be for driving home the theme of the message. If you haven't begun yet, the section below should help you get started.

Tips on Creating a Successful Drama Ministry

This book is designed specifically for use in church worship services — preaching to the choir, as it were — not to introduce the unchurched to spiritual truths (although many of the sketches might work for that purpose as well). For our purposes, it is best to think of how drama would work most effectively in your own church and where to get started. The information that follows deals with typical questions that may arise in getting your drama ministry off the ground. They are what I refer to as the seven Ps of an effective production.

The Players

Most of the original participants in these sketches were high school students — not because they were the only ones who might volunteer, but because they were my focus when starting out. Certainly after a few sketches I actually had other people in the congregation coming up and offering their services for subsequent dramas; there are more thespian

2

"wannabes" in your congregation than you know! I will tell you, however, that the main reason that I continue to use primarily youth in my productions is that they are very flexible and very willing to perform at a moment's notice. I have never asked for volunteer actors on a Sunday morning where I did not have at least twice as many hands go up as I had parts for. That kind of enthusiasm is hard to beat, and it certainly comes shining through in their performance. If you do use multi-generational casts, please try to remember that flexibility often disappears as cast members mature. Your practice times should be considerate of their particular place in the journey. It's been my experience that kids don't necessarily need much lead time while adults usually prefer it. Try, however, to find actors from all generations to perform these sketches. The more ages represented on the stage, the more people you will reach in the pews. But most of all, let the players in on the purpose so they can give themselves up to be a part of it. Your actors must have a certain believability in order for the production to be a success. Make sure that they are willing to attempt that. If they are, even if they don't pull it off, the sincere nature of the attempt will sell the congregation.

The Practice

Okay, time for soul-baring. I'm not as organized as I would like to be. Sometimes the drama gets distributed a week ahead of time, and sometimes it doesn't get written until early Sunday morning. Yes, right before the service. Somehow, God hasn't failed to send his muses in the nick of time, but I don't like to push my luck. The point is, often the practices for our sketches have happened only minutes before the service. The way our services are structured, we usually practice in the half-hour break between Sunday school and the worship service. While I don't necessarily advocate that you do this, it should be of some comfort to any director reading this that we have never had a problem with this approach, usually because the actors involved are familiar with the process and don't mind my M.O. If this is not the case for you, I would recommend that you set aside an hour during the week or on a Saturday evening to rehearse the sketch. This way you can have a good idea of any problems that may arise before you're in the middle of a "Sunday Morning Live" episode with no TelePrompTer.

Speaking of TelePrompTers, you may have guessed that if the

script doesn't get into the hands of the actors until minutes before they perform, it isn't likely to be memorized. While memorization is always preferred, it isn't always necessary to achieve an effective performance. Hiding scripts is a lost art. Pasting key dialog sections on the insides of magazines, taping them to the floor, hiding them on a benign-looking clipboard, even taped to the back of one of the characters (as long as he/she doesn't turn his/her back to the audience) ... all of these tricky little ways of avoiding memorization help the actors to be more natural on-stage and provide for a more effective delivery. Cheating? No, it's not cheating! It's creative theater. Okay, technically, it's cheating. Sue me.

The Properties

These sketches were designed to be as user-friendly as possible. For that reason, they hardly ever call for props that would not be found in your typical church storage closet. The few props that you will need are listed at the beginning of the sketch. More often than not, most things can be pantomimed. It often adds to the hilarity of the sketch. You'll rarely need special costumes. The staging is also very minimal by design. The more complicated your set becomes, the less effective the drama becomes in setting the mood of the service. For example, if you must have half the congregation help you move the ark (to scale) into place for the "Details, Details" sketch, and the other half helping you clean up the animals' accidents afterward, your timing is shot. Less is better in this instance. A chair strategically placed in the center of the stage is often all that's necessary to denote an entire church sanctuary. You'd be surprised, but when in doubt, underdo it.

The Purpose

You must never forget the reason that you are using drama in your service in the first place. Good drama complements the sermon theme and highlights what the pastor has in mind for the congregation to take home with them. For this reason it is a good idea to let your pastor see the script before the performance and to make suggestions as to additions or deletions that may be critical to the sketch achieving its purpose. This way he/she is also prepared to make comments on the sketch at some point in the sermon and tie it in to the theme of the day. It's not a bad idea to give your pastor a chance to pray about the performance with you as well (or without you, depending on what he/she thinks of the sketch!).

The Personalization

Every sketch in the book is designed with a certain theme in mind, but often there are places to tie in your own congregation to the action on the stage. For the sake of flexibility, many of the characters are gender-neutral. Change their names when necessary to fit your actors. Places to insert your congregation's name, your pastor's name, or some familiar things about a locality or local sports team often provide that key laugh that will make the sketch stick for one of your parishioners. If there is no spot to do that in the sketch you are working with that morning, I would suggest that you improvise and find a way to customize whenever you can. In fact, I don't mind if you change anything you want within the script — as long as you make it funnier or better in some way. Otherwise, I'll find some way to hunt you down and scold you for messing up my perfect sketch. Really. I mean it.

The Placement

This is the actual spot in the order of service during which the sketch will be performed. In our church, we find it most effective to perform the sketch as a prelude to the sermon, after the singing, call to worship, prayer, etc. I find that this helps to set the stage for the sermon that follows, especially if the pastor is in good communication with the drama coordinator. The transition can then be very smooth and relevant and allows the pastor a springboard for jumping into the message. Others prefer to have the sketch follow the sermon to drive the point home; once again, coordination is paramount. Wherever you place the sketch in the order of service, make certain that the pastor has the opportunity to tie the sketch and the sermon together, even if he/she opts not to take that opportunity. But if he/she doesn't, subtly try to encourage it. (Example: "Hey, pastor! Would it kill you to make reference to the sketch once in a while?" Or something like that.)

The Pilot

In all church drama teams, there must be a leader. In most dramatic productions, this person is known as the director. "Why not here?" you may ask. *Does director start with a P? No! Okay, then!* This is the person who oversees the production, directs the actors, and channels the request for a drama into the outcome of the production itself. This may vary from sketch to sketch, but there must be one individual that makes each mini-play fulfill its destiny. Since you are the person reading this, it may very well be you. If this is the case, and you are new to directing, here are a few helpful pointers as you work with the players in your production. To be cute (I have very few opportunities), I made sure they all start with the same letter. Here are the five Vs of direction.

Voice

Voice is very important. Oftentimes the things that are said are not nearly as important as the *way* they are said. You as the director are going to be much more likely to be in tune with the vision for the sketch than will your actors. When they say a line incorrectly, stop them. Read the line the way you think it was written to be said. If they learn it wrong by doing it wrong the first time without correction, they are much more likely to maintain that delivery in subsequent performances. Make sure that your characters do not deliver the lines flatly. Put a lilt in the dialog whenever possible — it makes it more real. Don't be afraid to change the wording to make it sound comfortable. If the actors come off as stiff, the message will be insincere as well. Encourage your actors to loosen up. Even though they are playing a part, they should try to make the character as believable and natural as possible.

Volume

Just as in business, the secret to the success of a good drama is often VOLUME, VOLUME, VOLUME! If the audience cannot hear the lines, it doesn't matter how funny they are—they won't laugh. Try to be as technology-friendly as you can; P.A. systems were built with drama in mind. Don't be afraid to put microphones in obvious locations — they won't distract as much as the lack of understanding by your audience will. Keep preaching to your actors to project. If you have to, buy a gigantic ear, put it next to your head, and yell "WHAT?!" whenever the volume seems to be lacking. They'll get the hint.

Velocity

This may be especially true of young actors, but when people are on-stage for the first time, they have a tendency to want to get it over with as soon as possible. Sometimes this can take the form of talking much too rapidly so that the lines get lost in the shuffle. In other instances, improperly timed lines can interrupt the flow of the dialog — it must feel natural in order for it to come off, but there must also be ample pauses for laughter when appropriate. If you don't say "Slow down" at least forty times in the first run-through of your first production, you're probably focusing on something else.

Visibility

Unless it is a commercial for blue jeans, it is a really poor practice to have your actors position themselves with their backs toward the audience. But this is not the only positioning faux pas (pronounced "big boo-boo"). In many small churches, the chancel area barely has room for a pulpit and sometimes a pastor, let alone the crew from *Oklahoma!* In order to effectively pull off a Sunday sketch, you may need to get creative. Try to always have your actors face the congregation — in a wrap-around setting, try to get them to spend equal time facing all audience members. It is important for the actors, if they are putting themselves into the sketch as much as they should be, to let their facial expressions be seen. The sketch is a very visual medium. (Or large, depending upon your cast size. Sorry. Can't resist a bad pun.) and if the congregation can't see the actions and reactions, they're missing most of the message. Be creative and practical and all will go well.

Vantage

I know that it may not be the same as if the sanctuary were full, but it is a good idea as a director to change your vantage point in various run-throughs. This will allow you to see the production as various members of the congregation will see it. It is a really good idea to sit in the very back on the second run-through. If you have any difficulty hearing with the sanctuary empty, think about how difficult it may be for the people to hear when it is full. This will also give you an idea of the visibility at various locations throughout the sanctuary, as well as give you an idea of how well the actors are getting the idea of connecting with the audience. The connection is only as good as the worst seat in the house.

Here are my suggestions on how to manage an effective production. Adapt, adopt, or abandon them as you see fit.

- Choose a sketch. (Kind of important or else rehearsal gets really confusing …)
- Distribute the sketch to recruited cast members.
- Set a rehearsal time.
- Be there. (Sets a good example for the cast members.)
- Explain the purpose/theme of sketch/service.
- First run-through. Make certain everyone knows all the words. (Not a joke — you'd be surprised.) If possible, check for proper vocal inflection and stresses. Make sure the actors read it the way you hear it when you read it to yourself. Trust your instinct.
- Second run-through. Move around. Check for how people will hear it from various locations. Emphasize volume on this run-through.
- Third run-through. Continue to change location, emphasizing visibility and pacing on this run-through. You may also want to decide how to disguise the scripts of those who do not feel comfortable with memorization.
- Fourth run-through. Possibly last, but most important: Try to keep your eye on all five Vs as you continue to move about the sanctuary. Actors are getting comfortable about this time, and you can check for how "real" they are feeling to the impartial audience member. This will probably have to be you, but it wouldn't hurt to ask someone else to give feedback.
- Final run-through, if necessary. Because the sketches are short, this will all take place in about forty-five minutes or so, even with goofing off. By the fifth run-through, you'll have a good idea of how the sketch will play on Sunday morning. Make certain that any necessary props or costumes have been assigned to cast members or otherwise arranged in advance. Thank everyone involved and tell them how great they have done, or they may not volunteer next time. (Note: This is a very important step!)

Keep in mind that drama is supposed to be fun. Entertaining, even. If you don't take steps to insure that it is, no one will want to perform the sketches, and no one will want to watch them, either. More importantly, you will have lost a valuable teaching tool for your congregation. And that is what this book is all about: being able to participate in a worship service with a smile. Have a lot of fun with it!

Daniel Wray

NOTE: The numerals running vertically down the left margin of each page of dialog are for the convenience of the director. With these, he/she may easily direct attention to a specific passage.

Absolutely, Positively ... Maybe!

A sketch about saying what we mean and meaning what we say.

Theme: Straight answers, honesty

Scripture References: Proverbs 16:11, 19:1, Matthew 5:33-37; Galatians 1:7

Synopsis: A customer tries to buy a car at a dealership and is baffled by the salesperson's doublespeak.

Cast: Salesperson
Customer

Props: A business card.

Setting: A new car dealership.

1   *(SALESPERSON is On-stage. CUSTOMER walks in.)*
2   **SALESPERSON:** Can I help you, sir?
3   **CUSTOMER:** Why, yes, I believe you can. I'd like to buy a new car.
4   **SALESPERSON:** Well, let me put your mind at ease! This is the
5   number one dealership for new cars on this entire block!
6   **CUSTOMER:** *(Confused)* But ... your dealership is the *only* thing
7   on this block.
8   **SALESPERSON:** Exactly. You think we'd have gotten so big by
9   NOT selling cars? Now, what are we in the market for?
10   **CUSTOMER:** Well, what is your specialty?
11   **SALESPERSON:** Depends on what you're looking for.
12   **CUSTOMER:** Why should that matter?
13   **SALESPERSON:** Because we want to get you the right car, now,
14   don't we?!
15   **CUSTOMER:** Yes, but ...
16   **SALESPERSON:** Now what can we put you in?
17   **CUSTOMER:** Well, what do you sell the most of?
18   **SALESPERSON:** Well, it depends ...
19   **CUSTOMER:** On?
20   **SALESPERSON:** On what kind of car you're looking for. Sports
21   coupe, family car, minivan ...?
22   **CUSTOMER:** Well, I was thinking of something sporty ...
23   **SALESPERSON:** What a coincidence! Our specialty!
24   **CUSTOMER:** *(Impressed)* **Really ...**
25   **SALESPERSON:** Yes, *(Gestures)* now over here is our brand new
26   1999 *(Insert current year.)* Ultra LX 2000.
27   **CUSTOMER:** 1999? We're barely into 1998. *(Insert current years.)*
28   **SALESPERSON:** See how progressive we are? Look at the lines,
29   look at the interior, look at the ...
30   **CUSTOMER:** *Price!* Great balls of fire!
31   **SALESPERSON:** Sir, we can finance you so easily, a man of your
32   income won't even feel it.
33   **CUSTOMER:** But you have no idea how much I make.
34   **SALESPERSON:** Oh, I can tell. But seriously, this car is worth it.
35   **CUSTOMER:** Well, I'm looking for something with certain

1	qualifications ...
2	SALESPERSON: You name it, this baby's got it!
3	CUSTOMER: Gas mileage?
4	SALESPERSON: Excellent!
5	CUSTOMER: Could you be a bit more specific?
6	SALESPERSON: What are you looking for?
7	CUSTOMER: Well, I'd like something that gets 30 ...
8	SALESPERSON: 34 city, 37 highway, if you drive it right ...
9	CUSTOMER: Which is ...
10	SALESPERSON: Exactly how you'll drive it, I'm sure ... *(Mumbles)*
11	coasting on hills, shutting it off at stoplights, *(Louder)* the
12	usual! What else are you looking for?
13	CUSTOMER: Something that's roomy enough ...
14	SALESPERSON: You could haul an eleven-piece pit group home
15	from the furniture store in the next block and not even know
16	it was in there!
17	CUSTOMER: Really?
18	SALESPERSON: Really. What else?
19	CUSTOMER: Well, I've had a few tickets, and I don't need any
20	more. This thing looks like it would draw tickets like a horse
21	draws flies.
22	SALESPERSON: Sir, if you get a ticket in this, I will personally pay
23	the fine.
24	CUSTOMER: What?
25	SALESPERSON: Would I lie to you? Now, let's talk financing. How
26	long would you like to have to pay the car off?
27	CUSTOMER: How long could I take?
28	SALESPERSON: Oh, as long as you'd like. A few years, perhaps.
29	CUSTOMER: A few? How many is a few?
30	SALESPERSON: Just a smidge over a couple. But not several.
31	CUSTOMER: So a few is like four or five.
32	SALESPERSON: If you'd like. Or more, if you'd like.
33	CUSTOMER: Wouldn't that be several?
34	SALESPERSON: Not really. But the closer you get to several, the
35	fewer dollars per month you'd pay.

1 CUSTOMER: What's the interest rate?
2 SALESPERSON: Not high.
3 CUSTOMER: How high?
4 SALESPERSON: Less than high.
5 CUSTOMER: So ... low?
6 SALESPERSON: Oh, yes, — low by comparison.
7 CUSTOMER: Comparison to what?
8 SALESPERSON: How old are you?
9 CUSTOMER: Twenty-seven. But why ...?
10 SALESPERSON: See? You're only twenty-seven and yet our interest
11   rate is nearly half your age!
12 CUSTOMER: Nearly half?
13 SALESPERSON: Well, relatively.
14 CUSTOMER: How relatively?
15 SALESPERSON: Well, let's say you had a birthday next month. If
16   you were then ...
17 CUSTOMER: *(Agitated) What exactly is your interest rate?!*
18 SALESPERSON: Exactly?
19 CUSTOMER: *Yes!*
20 SALESPERSON: I have no idea.
21 CUSTOMER: What?
22 SALESPERSON: See, it's based on the loan length and the amount
23   financed and ...
24 CUSTOMER: Look — stop. Let's try this. *(Pause)* Let's say I
25   wanted to put a thousand dollars down and have my pay-
26   ments be less than three hundred dollars per month for five
27   years. *Can you do this?!*
28 SALESPERSON: Absolutely.
29 CUSTOMER: Really?
30 SALESPERSON: Positively.
31 CUSTOMER: You're sure?
32 SALESPERSON: I am pretty certain.
33 CUSTOMER: A-ha!
34 SALESPERSON: Fairly sure.
35 CUSTOMER: How sure?

1   SALESPERSON: Well, it's the lease I can do.

2   CUSTOMER: *(Pause)* Did you say lease?

3   SALESPERSON: Based on a sixty-month lease with limited
4   mileage and payments of two hundred ninety-nine dollars per
5   month with a thousand dollars down excluding MSRP and
6   pro-rated to invoice value based on mileage ... sign here.

7   CUSTOMER: Now, just a minute! At the end of five years, what am
8   I left with?

9   SALESPERSON: A wonderful experience!

10   CUSTOMER: But no car.

11   SALESPERSON: Well, of course you have.

12   CUSTOMER: How so?

13   SALESPERSON: You have this car.

14   CUSTOMER: After the lease?

15   SALESPERSON: Of course.

16   CUSTOMER: For how much?

17   SALESPERSON: Well, that depends.

18   CUSTOMER: *Aarrggh!* Forget it! I don't need a car. I'll ... I'll turn
19   Amish and drive a buggy before I get a straight answer out
20   of you!

21   SALESPERSON: What?

22   CUSTOMER: *(Turns to leave.)* Good-bye!

23   SALESPERSON: Wait! *(CUSTOMER pauses as SALESPERSON*
24   *gives him a business card.)* If you're serious about this conver-
25   sion thing, look up my brother Sal. He sells buggies over on
26   Forty-third Street. He'll make you a sweet deal!

27   CUSTOMER: *Aarrggh!* *(Exits.)*

28   SALESPERSON: *(To audience)* It's getting so a man can't make an
29·   honest living anymore ... *(Exits.)*

30

31

32

33

34

35

And the Winner Is...

A sketch about the submission question.

Theme: Submission, marriage, relationships

Scripture Reference: Ephesians 5:21-33

Synopsis: A boxing match, in which the combatants are husband and wife, is the forum for a discussion on the true meaning of submission.

Cast: Announcer
Wife
Husband
Cheering Spectators (Optional)

Props: Bible.

Sound Effects: Cheering, bell.

Setting: A boxing ring.

1   *(ANNOUNCER takes his place at a lectern to the side. HUSBAND*
2   *and WIFE go to Center Stage. They appear to be ready to do bat-*
3   *tle — they dance around, shadow box, etc., as the announcer, who*
4   *is also the referee, opens with the introductions.)*
5 **ANNOUNCER:** *(In a high monotone announcer's voice)* **Good**
6   **evening, ladies and gentlemen, and welcome to the oldest**
7   **conflict in the history of the world!** *(If possible, plant some*
8   *spectators on the front row to cheer when appropriate. They cheer.*
9   *Pause)* **In this corner, weighing in at …** *(Looks over at WIFE,*
10   *who is shaking her head "no" slowly.)* **OK, we'll skip that part**
11   **…** *(Pause for laugh)* **… armed only with her intellect** *(Brief*
12   *pause)* **and the scriptural reference of Ephesians 5:21-33 …**
13   *(Same draw out for effect)* **the wife!** *(Crowd may cheer —*
14   *mostly women.)* **And in this corner, armed also with his intellect**
15   *(Pause while the announcer rolls his eyes and the husband mim-*
16   *ics like he's smart)* **and the scriptural reference of Ephesians**
17   **5:21-33 …** *(Draw out the last three for effect)* **the husband!**
18   *(Again, crowd may cheer—mostly men. ANNOUNCER pauses*
19   *and then motions or calls both of them into the center of the ring.)*
20   **All right, let's have a clean fight. No whining, no complaining,**
21   **no bringing up things that happened prior to 1989.** *(Pause)* **No**
22   **toothpaste lid remarks, no comments about shopping habits,**
23   **and absolutely no toilet-seat references. Are these rules clear?**
24   *(Both nod.)* **All right, now let's have a good, clean fight.**
25   **Remember, it's winner take all, loser sleeps on the hide-a-bed.**
26   **Now, shake hands.** *(They do.)* **Go to your corners and when the**
27   **bell rings, come out fighting.** *(They go to opposite corners and*
28   *wait. When the bell rings, they approach each other, fists up.)*
29 **WIFE:** **Well, go on. You know what you're gonna do — take your**
30   **best shot.**
31 **HUSBAND:** **All right, I will. Right in verse twenty-two — "Wives,**
32   **submit to your husbands as to the LORD!"**
33 **WIFE:** **Yeah? Well, in the version I have, taken from the original**
34   **language, it says "Wives, understand and support your hus-**
35   **bands in ways that show your support for Christ"** *(Ephesians*

1   *5:22, TM).* I think I do a pretty good job of that!

2   HUSBAND: Yeah?

3   WIFE: Yeah. Besides, the passage goes on to say, "Husbands, love

4   your wives, just as Christ loves the church and gave himself

5   up for her" *(Ephesians 5:25).*

6   HUSBAND: OK, OK. I can handle that. I love you, you know that.

7   WIFE: Yeah, but how about the part where you give yourself up

8   for me?

9   HUSBAND: I think my version says something else...

10   WIFE: Oh yeah? Like what?

11   HUSBAND: *(Stumbling around)* Uh … like … uh … wives, submit to

12   your husbands … .

13   ANNOUNCER: Sorry, you already threw that punch — come on,

14   come on — let's mix it up a little …

15   WIFE: And the passage goes on to say that you should love your

16   wife so much that you become one flesh. What about that?

17   HUSBAND: Uh … yeah. Uh … *(Pause)* I love you!

18   WIFE: You already said that.

19   HUSBAND: Well, I do. *(Stern look from the ANNOUNCER)* All right,

20   all right. Uh, doesn't it say somewhere in there that wives are

21   to respect their husbands?

22   WIFE: Yes it does. I respect you. Most of the time … but the verse starts

23   out that men must love their wives as much as themselves …

24   HUSBAND: What are you saying?

25   WIFE: What do you think I'm saying?

26   HUSBAND: Oh, I know what you're saying.

27   WIFE: I'm not saying anything.

28   HUSBAND: Oh, you're saying plenty …

29   ANNOUNCER: *Hey, Hey, Hey!* There'll be none of that dirty fight-

30   ing in this ring. Get back to the argument.

31   WIFE: Well?

32   HUSBAND: Well … *(Pause)* Well, I do love you as much as me. I

33   don't love myself *nearly* as much as I love you.

34   WIFE: Oh really? Do your actions say that?

35   HUSBAND: Well, I hope so … don't they?

1 WIFE: Well, most of the time. But I support you, too, like it says in
2   verse twenty-two.
3 HUSBAND: Yeah? Well, you don't always completely trust decisions
4   that I make — how is that being submissive?
5 WIFE: Not always — but even when I disagree, I still support you.
6 HUSBAND: Yeah? *(Pause)* Well, I think it's important that the first
7   thing the passage starts off with is, "Wives, submit to your
8   husbands!"
9 ANNOUNCER: That's another warning!
10 HUSBAND: Sorry.
11 WIFE: But the passage doesn't start off that way — it starts by say-
12   ing that out of respect to God, that we should be reverent to
13   one another — verse twenty-one.
14 HUSBAND: Really?
15 WIFE: Yes, really. And it goes on to say that you are to treat me the
16   way that Christ treats the church — to bring out the best in
17   me so that I can support you as best I can.
18 HUSBAND: *(Grabs Bible and pauses, while reading.)* But it does say,
19   "Wives, submit to your husbands ..."
20 WIFE: Honey, I'm beginning to think you read this passage like you
21   read the directions on how to put together Nathan's bike. You
22   read one line and think you know the whole thing ...
23 HUSBAND: Hey! *(Turning to the announcer)* I thought you said no
24   cheap shots!
25 ANNOUNCER: *(He shrugs.)* I did, but I *liked* that one. *(As he is*
26   *arguing with the ANNOUNCER, WIFE sneaks in a sucker punch*
27   *and the HUSBAND goes down. The ANNOUNCER steps in and*
28   *starts counting to eight.)*
29 WIFE: And if you had read the passage, you would have read the
30   part where the husband provides leadership to the wife — not
31   by domineering, but by cherishing. Just as Christ cherishes
32   the church. *(The HUSBAND rises to his feet.)*
33 HUSBAND: All right, all right already. I give up.
34 WIFE: So do I.
35 HUSBAND: I'm going to reread and learn exactly what the

1   Scripture says I'm supposed to do.

2   **WIFE: Wow. Wouldn't that be a little too much like asking for**

3   **directions?**

4   **HUSBAND: Hey — that's a cheap shot.**

5   **WIFE: Yup!**

6   **ANNOUNCER: We have a winner!** *(He raises both of their arms*

7   *simultaneously, then all exit.)*

Anger-Be-Gone!

A sketch about overcoming anger.

Theme: Anger

**Scripture
Reference:**   Matthew 5:21

Synopsis: Two drivers fight over a parking space until they are sprayed with a new product. All of a sudden, the scenario plays out much differently!

Cast: Driver 1
Driver 2
Announcer

Props: Aerosol can with a label saying "Anger-Be-Gone."

Setting: A parking lot.

1   *(ANNOUNCER stands off to the side, holding aerosol can. DRIVERS*
2   *1 & 2 pantomime driving toward each other, presumably for the*
3   *same parking spot.)*
4   **DRIVER 2: Hey, jerk! I was going to park there!**
5   **DRIVER 1: Yeah? Well, both of us won't fit!**
6   **DRIVER 2: Yeah, but I saw it first!**
7   **DRIVER 1: Oh, really! That would explain how come I'm sitting in it!**
8   **DRIVER 2: I only stopped because I thought you were going to go**
9   **straight!**
10   **DRIVER 1: Well, I wasn't! I was heading for *my* parking spot ...**
11   **DRIVER 2: Oh yeah?** *(DRIVERS 1 & 2 continue to pantomime argu-*
12   *ing over the parking place as the ANNOUNCER begins.)*
13   **ANNOUNCER:** *(In a very exaggerated announcer's voice)* **Does this**
14   **look familiar? How many times have you gotten angry with**
15   **someone and wished there was an easy resolution to the**
16   **problem? Well, now there is!** *(Holds up an aerosol can that has*
17   *been relabeled "Anger-Be-Gone.")* **Introducing new Anger-Be-**
18   **Gone! That's right, this handy little spray will solve all your**
19   **problems! No more going to bed angry! No more unresolved**
20   **disputes with your neighbor! No more fights with your in-laws!**
21   **Now all you need is Anger-Be-Gone! Arguing about politics?**
22   **Give a little spray! How about those annoying sales calls? Just**
23   **keep it near the phone, and your anger will disappear like**
24   **magic! That's right! Just watch!** *(The ANNOUNCER sprays*
25   *toward DRIVERS 1 & 2 and they immediately stop arguing.)*
26   **DRIVER 1: Hey, you know what? You take the spot. I'll park out**
27   **on the street. I don't mind!**
28   **DRIVER 2: What? Don't be ridiculous! You *were* here first. Just**
29   **keep the spot! I'll find another one!**
30   **DRIVER 1: Hey, I'm really sorry! I don't know what I was thinking!**
31   **DRIVER 2: Hey, forget about it! I'm the one who's sorry!**
32   **DRIVER 1: Hey — how 'bout I buy you lunch?**
33   **DRIVER 2: Sounds good to me!** *(They exit with arms around each*
34   *other's shoulders.)*
35   **ANNOUNCER: That's right! Anger disappears like magic! So**

1   **don't delay! Get your Anger-Be-Gone today! Available wher-**
2   **ever fine prayers are answered!**
3
4
5
6
7
8
9
10
11
12
13
14
15
16
17
18
19
20
21
22
23
24
25
26
27
28
29
30
31
32
33
34
35

Are We There Yet?

A sketch on the difficulty of living peacefully.

Theme: Peace

**Scripture
Reference:**   1 Peter 3:8-11

Synopsis: When a family experiences a little too much togetherness on a road trip, the father must continually remind himself to deal with exasperating situations peacefully.

Cast: Father
Mother
Son
Daughter

Props: None.

Setting: The family car, while on vacation.

1   *(The family stands at Center Stage, arranged as if riding in a car.*
2   *MOTHER and FATHER stand in front, with FATHER pantomim-*
3   *ing driving. SON and DAUGHTER stand behind them, in the back*
4   *seat. If possible, the actors should be moving at all times, to sim-*
5   *ulate car movement from place to place. Ideally, they should have*
6   *an obstacle of some kind to move entirely behind periodically to*
7   *simulate the transitions between different portions of the trip; cir-*
8   *cling behind a curtain barely wider than the group itself is*
9   *preferred. The four people should begin slowly shuffling across*
10   *stage. The kids should be typically annoying to each other and*
11   *should pantomime bothering each other throughout the sketch.)*
12 **FATHER: Honey, I really think this vacation was a great idea!**
13 **MOTHER: Well, when I heard the way you'd been snapping our**
14   **heads off, I knew we had to do something!**
15 **FATHER: I know. It just all seems to get to me sometimes. I mean, in**
16   **our Bible study we've been studying First Peter, and there's a**
17   **verse there that just bothers me. You know, about living at**
18   **peace with all men, so much as it depends upon me. I don't seem**
19   **to have a good handle on doing that at home or at work ...**
20 **SON: Cut it out!**
21 **DAUGHTER: What?!**
22 **FATHER:** *(Chuckles.)* **Hey, you kids! Both of you! Let's not start out**
23   **our vacation this way, or it's gonna be a long trip!**
24 **SON: She started it!**
25 **DAUGHTER: I did not! You know I didn't!**
26 **FATHER:** *(Angrily)* **Hey, look!**
27 **MOTHER: Honey ...**
28 **FATHER:** *(Calming down, with a nervous chuckle)* **What I mean is, I**
29   **don't really care who started it, just please stop.** *(They begin to*
30   *move near the partition they will disappear behind.)* **Now, where**
31   **was I?**
32 **MOTHER: You were about to explode.**
33 **FATHER:** *(Laughing)* **Now, dear, I know that I may have had a tem-**
34   **per in the past, but I really think I can live at peace with**
35   **others. And I'm starting with you guys, all right?**

1   MOTHER: Well, we'll see. I just hope we can get there without
2   killing each other.
3   FATHER: No problem! I am at peace with all men! *(They exit behind*
4   *a partition, with kids fighting each other. Coming from behind the*
5   *partition, FATHER is obviously annoyed, but remains looking*
6   *straight ahead with a forced smile on his face during the trip*
7   *across the stage.)*
8   SON: You wart-hog!
9   DAUGHTER: Pea-brain!
10   SON: Pizza-face!
11   DAUGHTER: Motor mouth!
12   SON: Llama breath!
13   DAUGHTER: Poodle hair!
14   SON: Airhead!
15   DAUGHTER: Double dip!
16   SON: Junior mint!
17   DAUGHTER: *(Long pause)* What?!
18   FATHER: *(Under his breath)* I am at peace with all men!
19   MOTHER: Honey, have you always had that little bulging vein on
20   the side of your head? *(All exit with FATHER still not looking at*
21   *anyone. After slight pause, all enter again, going the other way.*
22   *FATHER keeps the same even-keel demeanor with slight voice*
23   *variations, while the kids try to make theirs sound exactly alike.)*
24   DAUGHTER and SON: *(In unison)* Are we there yet, Dad?
25   FATHER: No.
26   DAUGHTER and SON: *(In unison)* Are we there yet, Dad?
27   FATHER: No.
28   DAUGHTER and SON: *(In unison)* Are we there yet, Dad?
29   FATHER: No.
30   DAUGHTER and SON: *(In unison)* Are we there yet, Dad?
31   FATHER: No.
32   DAUGHTER and SON: *(In unison)* Are we there yet, Dad?
33   FATHER: No! *(All exit with FATHER still not looking at anyone. After*
34   *slight pause, all enter again, going the other way.)*
35   MOTHER: You know, we should have taken that interchange back

1   there if we wanted to see the Grand Canyon.

2   FATHER: I know the way. We've been there before.

3   MOTHER: But the map says that it would be much quicker to go
4   that way.

5   FATHER: *(Under his breath)* I am at peace with all men! *(Pause)* The
6   map is wrong.

7   MOTHER: Let's just stop and ask for directions.

8   FATHER: I don't need directions.

9   MOTHER: Well, then let *me* stop and ask for directions.

10   FATHER: *You* don't need directions.

11   MOTHER: Why don't I need directions if I want directions?

12   FATHER: You're not driving.

13   MOTHER: Then *you* ask for directions!

14   FATHER: I don't need directions.

15   MOTHER: Would it kill you to ask for directions?

16   FATHER: *(Pauses, then looks straight at MOTHER in a deadpan stare*
17   *with no emotion.)* Yes. *(Pause)* It would kill me to ask for direc-
18   tions. *(All exit with FATHER still not looking at anyone. After*
19   *slight pause, all enter again, going the other way.)*

20   DAUGHTER: Dad, I need to go to the bathroom!

21   FATHER: You just went.

22   DAUGHTER: When?

23   FATHER: Before we left.

24   DAUGHTER: That was two hundred miles ago!

25   FATHER: What's your point?

26   DAUGHTER: I need to go to the bathroom!

27   FATHER: I can go three hundred miles before I need to …

28   MOTHER: Oh, brother! Let's not play "Name that Bladder Capacity"
29   again!

30   SON: Why not? It's better than highway alphabet!

31   DAUGHTER: I need to go!

32   MOTHER: Honey, let's stop. I need to go, too.

33   FATHER: You just went.

34   MOTHER: Dear, if we don't stop soon, it will be too late!

35   FATHER: *(Gritting teeth)* I am at peace with all men!

1   DAUGHTER: *I need to go!*
2   FATHER: All right! *(Pause, taking deep breath)* All right. We'll stop
3   at the next exit. *(Under his breath)* I am at peace with all men!
4   *(All exit behind partition. From behind the partition, the follow-*
5   *ing dialog can be heard.)*
6   DAUGHTER: Thanks a lot, Dad! I probably have permanent
7   system problems now!
8   MOTHER: It's about time we stopped, dear! I wish you would be a
9   little more compassionate toward your family!
10   SON: I need more money, Dad! That last Slurpee spilled all over the
11   backseat.
12   FATHER: *(Under his breath)* I am at peace with all men!
13   DAUGHTER: Dad, let's just go home! *(Pause)* Dad? *(Pause)* Dad?!
14   *(There is a slight pause before FATHER appears, alone, driving*
15   *back across the stage, smiling.)*
16   FATHER: *(Singing)* I've got peace like a river, I've got peace like a
17   river … *(FATHER exits behind the partition.)*
18
19
20
21
22
23
24
25
26
27
28
29
30
31
32
33
34
35

Ask Doctor Donna

A sketch on biblical truth.

Theme:	Scriptural truth
Scripture References:	Matthew 7:20, Acts 17:11, 2 Timothy 3:6-7, John 7:40-43, Jude 4
Synopsis:	Doctor Donna freely dispenses advice on her radio talk show. She claims it's scriptural — but is it?
Cast:	Doctor Donna Caller 1 (Off-stage Voice) Caller 2 (Off-stage Voice) Caller 3 (Off-stage Voice) Caller 4 (Off-stage Voice)
Props:	Headphones, push-button telephone.
Setting:	A talk radio studio. Place a table and chair at Center Stage.

1   (*Doctor Donna sits at the table with headphones on. She should*
2   *have a phone with buttons to push in front of her. She takes calls*
3   *from callers and answers questions definitively, with sometimes*
4   *less-than-definitive answers. Callers are heard but not seen.*)
5   DR. DONNA: OK, we're back from commercial, and you're here with
6   Doctor Donna on *Nothing But the Truth*, your daily question-
7   and-answer show. Today we're taking questions on everything
8   under the sun, so if you have a question, and you need the
9   truth, give us a call. Remember our slogan, "Go ahead and
10   ask; we're never wrong!" All our lines are full, let's go to
11   Monica on line one. Hello, Monica, you're on the air.
12   CALLER 1: Hello? Am I on?
13   DR. DONNA: (*Annoyed*) Yes, Monica. What's your question?
14   CALLER 1: Oh, wow! I didn't think I'd get on!
15   DR. DONNA: Well you won't be on long if you don't have a
16   question ...
17   CALLER 1: Oh, right. Yes. Well, I am a first-time caller but a long-
18   time listener, and I know that you're big into truth, but I'm
19   wanting to know — do you always base your decisions on
20   scriptural truth?
21   DR. DONNA: Well, I try to. What's your question?
22   CALLER 1: Well, I have a neighbor who has been out of work for
23   quite a while, and we've been helping out whenever we can,
24   but I just wanted to know how much we really need to do so
25   that we don't feel guilty.
26   DR. DONNA: OK, you say your neighbor hasn't been working?
27   CALLER 1: Right.
28   DR. DONNA: For how long?
29   CALLER 1: Oh, I'd say it's been a little less than a year ...
30   DR. DONNA: A year? I'd say you're done.
31   CALLER 1: Really?
32   DR. DONNA: Really.
33   CALLER 1: But I know that our pastor has been talking about how
34   the Bible tells us to love our neighbors as ourselves, and I
35   would never let my own family go hungr ...

1   DR. DONNA: Well, the Bible also says that God helps those who
2   help themselves … right?
3   CALLER 1: Actually, I don't think that's in the Bible …
4   DR. DONNA: Sure it is! I think it's in Hezekiah somewhere.
5   CALLER 1: Really?
6   DR. DONNA: Of course. Remember, we're never wrong! Thanks
7   for your call. *(Pause)* You're here with Doctor Donna on
8   *Nothing But the Truth*. Hello, caller?
9   CALLER 2: Yes, Doctor Donna?
10   DR. DONNA: Yes. Go ahead, you're on the air.
11   CALLER 2: Yes, well I was wondering, I have a couple of rental
12   properties, and I'd like to get one of my tenants out because
13   he's not very neat.
14   DR. DONNA: Well, legally you might have your hands full …
15   CALLER 2: Well, the lease is up, it's just that I know I shouldn't let
16   him go just for that …
17   DR. DONNA: Why not?
18   CALLER 2: Well, it doesn't seem like the most compassionate thing
19   to do. I'm a Christian, and I don't think that's what Jesus
20   would do …
21   DR. DONNA: Oh, he might. You said your tenant was really
22   messy, right?
23   CALLER 2: Yeah. …
24   DR. DONNA: Well, cleanliness is next to godliness, so if he's not
25   being that clean, God is probably on your side.
26   CALLER 2: Is that in the Bible?
27   DR. DONNA: Oh, sure! It's in Proverbs — I think. Anyway, let the
28   bum go with a clear conscience.
29   CALLER 2: Oh. OK. *(Pause)* Thanks …
30   DR. DONNA: You're listening to Doctor Donna on *Nothing But the
31   Truth*. We have one open line, and we're taking your calls. Let's
32   go to Francis in Oakdale. Hello, Francis, you're on the air.
33   CALLER 3: Yes, Doctor, I've been listening and I thought I'd call
34   because you always seem to give such good advice based upon
35   scriptural principles.

1 DR. DONNA: Go ahead — what's your question?
2 CALLER 3: Well, my wife and I have some friends of ours over
3 every week. We really like them, and we usually have a great
4 time …
5 DR. DONNA: So what's your question?
6 CALLER 3: Well, it's their kids. They are a bit more rambunctious
7 than our kids, and we really don't feel comfortable telling
8 them to quiet down, but their parents won't.
9 DR. DONNA: Uh-huh. Can I ask you a question?
10 CALLER 3: Sure.
11 DR. DONNA: Exactly when did you have the spine-removal
12 surgery done?
13 CALLER 3: What?
14 DR. DONNA: It's your house, isn't it?
15 CALLER 3: Well … yeah, but they're not my ki —
16 DR. DONNA: I don't care whose kids they are — the Bible says that
17 kids should be seen and not heard, right?
18 CALLER 3: It does?
19 DR. DONNA: *(Pause)* Hello?!? Are you reading the Bible?
20 CALLER 3: Yeah. I guess I just didn't think that was in there.
21 DR. DONNA: Sure it is. I think it's in Hesitations. Anyhoo, let me
22 know what you decide to do. Next caller. You're on with
23 Doctor Donna on *Nothing But the Truth*, Mitch.
24 CALLER 4: Uh, yeah. Doctor Donna?
25 DR. DONNA: Yes, go ahead.
26 CALLER 4: Well, I've been listening all afternoon, and it seems to
27 me that you may be spouting forth some inaccuracies that
28 your listeners may be taking as truth.
29 DR. DONNA: They are truth. This is *Nothing but the Truth*,
30 after all …
31 CALLER 4: Yes, well, you've given references to books of the Bible
32 that don't exist for Scriptures that aren't there.
33 DR. DONNA: I have not. You must have been listening wrong.
34 CALLER 3: I really wish that were true. But a lot of the things
35 you've been giving as advice are nothing more than favorite

1   quotations. They're not from the Bible, they're from people.

2 DR. DONNA: Sir, I think you may be mistaken. I'm never wrong.

3 CALLER 4: Well, *that* may be inaccurate as well.

4 DR. DONNA: Are you serious?

5 CALLER 4: Yes, I'm serious. I think you started off with good

6   intentions, but your pride may be getting in your way. And as

7   the Bible tells us, "Pride goeth before destruction." So be care-

8   ful, Doctor Donna ...

9 DR. DONNA: I thought it was pride goeth before a fall, Mr. Smarty

10   Scripture! And I am well aware of the danger of being pride-

11   ful. It's one of the seven deadly sins mentioned in the Old

12   Testament.

13 CALLER 4: Well, once again, that's not accurate. There's really no

14   mention of seven deadly sins anywhere in the Scriptures. See,

15   you're taking worldly values and equating them with scrip-

16   tural truths. You can't do that.

17 DR. DONNA: Well, I never! I think you have too much spare time

18   on your hands, young man! And we all know that idle hands

19   are the devil's workshop. Now are you going to tell me that's

20   not scriptural?

21 CALLER 4: Well, actually ... it's not.

22 DR. DONNA: Well, we're nearly out of time for today. Do you have

23   any questions, or are you just going to continue to refuse to

24   believe that I know what I'm talking about?

25 CALLER 4: Well, if I did offer anything, I think it might just be

26   casting my pearls before swine at this point ...

27 DR. DONNA: Young man, are you calling me a swine?

28 CALLER 4: No, ma'am! It's from Matthew. It means that I'm

29   wasting my time.

30 DR. DONNA: And speaking of time, we're all out! Join us next time,

31   when we screen our callers a little better. Remember, we're

32   never wrong on *Nothing But the Truth*. Until next time, this is

33   Doctor Donna, hoping all your advice is as good as mine. Bye

34   for now!

35

The Battle Within

A sketch looking at inner turmoil
and how to deal with that suffering.

Theme: Suffering

Scripture Reference: 1 Peter 3:13, 14

Synopsis: This sketch is pantomimed by the actor while it is read Off-stage or taped and played over the sound system, giving the impression that we can hear Mr. Johnson's disparaging thoughts while waiting for a conference with his work supervisor.

Cast: Mr. Johnson (or Ms. Johnson)
Voice (Off-stage)

Props: None.

Setting: The workplace — just outside the boss's office Place a chair at Center Stage.

1	This sketch is non-spoken and non-memorized. All action takes
2	place On-stage with a taped accompaniment, listed below. The
3	actor should focus on the words that he/she will tape beforehand
4	to become familiar with movements and emotive expression.
5	*(Scene opens with MR./MS. JOHNSON sitting on a chair, at*
6	*his/her workplace, outside the boss's office. He/she is waiting for*
7	*an interview with his/her supervisor and is nervous. During the*
8	*scene he/she may pace, look at watch, etc. Whatever is done is*
9	*obviously designed to pass the time more quickly. His/her*
10	*thoughts are heard over the speaker.)*
11	**MR. JOHNSON: I wonder what's taking so long. My appointment**
12	**was for ten minutes ago.** *(Pause)* **I hate these kind of situa-**
13	**tions. I mean, I need the raise and all. I deserve the raise. I**
14	**work harder than anyone else here. When I took this job, I**
15	**knew it didn't pay all that well. But I know it's what God**
16	**wants me to be doing; he's proven that time and time again.**
17	*(Pause)* **Dad may have been right. I should've taken that job**
18	**with the State Department. It paid twice what this does … and**
19	**I'd have more time to spend with my family. Surely THAT**
20	**wouldn't have been out of God's will, would it?**
21	**"You're an idiot if you take a job with a ministry!" he said.**
22	**"God wants you to provide for your family, doesn't he?"**
23	*(Pause to walk)* **What's taking so long? I want to get this**
24	**over with.** *(Pause)* **Maybe if Jennifer hadn't had so many**
25	**problems when she was born — at least we wouldn't still have**
26	**that hospital bill hanging over our heads. And now with**
27	**another little one on the way …** *(Pause)* **I think if he says no**
28	**on the raise, I'm going to have to find something else. Some-**
29	**thing with better insurance. Ha. That could be anywhere.**
30	**God? Why do you do this to people who obviously seek your**
31	**will?** *(Pause)* **I think I'm going to have to quit. My stomach**
32	**can't take much more of this worrying about finances. I'm**
33	**tired of fighting it. I mean …** *(Pause)* **OK, God, if you want me**
34	**to keep this job — if this is really where I'm supposed to be —**
35	**I'd better get this raise.** *(Pause as he thinks about what he has*

1   *just said.)* **Heh-heh. So it comes to this. Blackmailing God. I**
2   **wonder if that's ever worked.** *(Pause)* **I'm so tired.**
3   *(Pause)* **My yoke is easy, my burden is light. Whoa —**
4   **where in the world did that come from? My burden is not**
5   **light.** *(Pause)* **Still, where did that thought come from? Is that**
6   **you, God?** *(Pause)* **Wait a minute, there was another verse —**
7   **at Bible study, in First Peter — what was it? "If you suffer for**
8   **what is right, you are blessed** (1 Peter 3:14, author's para-
9   phrase)." *(Pause)* **If you suffer, you are blessed.** *(Pause)* **I could**
10   **do with just a little less blessing right now, God.** *(Pause)* **Seri-**
11   **ously, why did I think of that verse?** *(Pause)* **Perhaps my**
12   **prayers have been a bit weary lately … maybe I need to give**
13   **this suffering and worry over to Somebody who's a little**
14   **better equipped to handle it.** *(Long pause as he bows head as if*
15   *praying.)* **OK, God, if you really want me to rest in you, that's**
16   **what I'll do. I'd appreciate it if you could drop a few verses in**
17   **the bill collectors' ears.**
18   **VOICE OFF-STAGE: Mr Johnson? The boss will see you now.**
19   *(MR. JOHNSON walks Off-stage.)*
20
21
22
23
24
25
26
27
28
29
30
31
32
33
34
35

Blessed Are the Suburbanites

A sketch looking at what the Sermon on the Mount says to us today.

Theme: Sermon on the Mount, Christian character

Scripture References: Matthew 5:1-12, Galatians 5:21, 22

Synopsis: Two neighbors discuss the Beatitudes while trying to maintain control of their "spirited" kids.

Cast: John
Dave

Props: None.

Setting: A back yard barbeque. Place a lawn chair at Center Stage for Dave.

1   *(DAVE is lounging on a chair while JOHN is flipping burgers on*
2   *an imaginary grill. The back yard is in front of them, so that lines*
3   *said to their Off-stage misbehaving children are directed at the*
4   *congregation. Many lines are interrupted. Timing is critical to the*
5   *humor of the piece.)*
6   JOHN: Dave, I'm sure glad you and the family could come over and
7   spend some time with us today. Sometimes it seems we get so
8   busy and don't take the time.
9   DAVE: Thanks for inviting us. The kids always have such a good
10   time together ...
11   JOHN: Yeah, just look at th — *(Noticing the kids misbehaving)*
12   Mitchell! Get off the lawnmower — NOW! It's not a toy!
13   *(Pause)* I don't care who got on it first — get off!
14   DAVE: Stay off the mower, Steven! *(Pause)* Yeah, it does feel good
15   to see you guys outside of church and to just relax a little.
16   JOHN: Absolutely. How do you like your steak?
17   DAVE: Medium is great. So, how are things at work?
18   JOHN: Oh, they're not bad. A little unfair, but I guess ... *(Pause —*
19   *to his kid again)* Mitchell, put the cat down! *(Pause)* I don't
20   care what it looks like, his tail is not a handle!
21   DAVE: How do you mean, unfair? *(Pause)* Steven, didn't he just say
22   not to pick the cat up by his tail? *(Pause)* Well, he meant either
23   one of you!
24   JOHN: Well, I just got passed by for a promotion, and I know I was
25   more deserving than the guy that got it.
26   DAVE: That's too bad. I guess we never stop realizing that life
27   isn't fair.
28   JOHN: Yeah, I suppose. I'm just having a tough time accepting it.
29   DAVE: I understand that. It's tough when you look at it through the
30   world's eyes.
31   JOHN: The world's eyes? What do you mean?
32   DAVE: I mean that it's perfectly natural to ... *(To child)* Steven! Get
33   off of him! Well, he can't breathe, that's why! *(Pause)* Because
34   he's BLUE! Now get off!
35   JOHN: He turns that color sometimes ...

1   DAVE: Yeah, well, anyway, I was saying that it's natural to want to
2   get what we deserve, but that's not always what is best for us
3   in God's plan.
4   JOHN: Oh, yeah?
5   DAVE: Look at the Beatitudes. Blessed are the poor in spirit,
6   blessed are those who mourn, blessed are those who are
7   persecuted. Doesn't say anything about how blessed the CEOs
8   of the world should be.
9   JOHN: Yeah, I suppose. But don't you think that when Jesus said
10   all those things, he was really just throwing out a bone to
11   those who were suffering? To let us know that something
12   better was around the corner?
13 DAVE: I don't think so. I used to. But the more you read the passage,
14   the more it becomes pretty clear that those are the qualities
15   that God values — the things he really wants us to strive for.
16 JOHN: So what does that mean for ... *(To child)* You know, if I
17   have to come out there and take you off of that shed myself,
18   there's going to be trouble, mister! *(Back to DAVE)* They
19   have a great time together, don't they?
20 DAVE: They sure do.
21 JOHN: Anyway, what does that mean for my situation? According
22   to the Scripture, I should be the lowest one on the totem pole
23   and be happy about it.
24 DAVE: Well, I suppose you could look at it that way. But I think
25   what Jesus is really trying to say is that you should adopt the
26   right attitude ...
27 JOHN: Or beatitude, as it were ...
28 DAVE: Yeah, cute. Anyway, if you have the servant approach to
29   things, then you'll be a happier individual, whether you get
30   the raise or not.
31 JOHN: Well, that seems easy enough to say, but isn't that just the
32   opposite of everything the world teaches?
33 DAVE: Yes, it is. But I believe that ... *(To child)* Steven! Where did
34   you get that rope? *(Pause)* I don't care, take it off of your sister!
35   *(Pause)* Anyway, I think that God wants us to strive for things

1   that are the opposite of what the world wants. "Lay not up for
2   yourselves ..."
3   JOHN: Oh, I know you're right. It's just a little difficult to keep
4   that perspective sometimes.
5   DAVE: You're telling me. There's not a day that goes by that I don't
6   need to remind myself. *(Pause)* How's the food coming?
7   JOHN: Well, in keeping with the theme, "Blessed are the hungry,
8   for they shall be filled!"
9   DAVE: Amen and amen. *(Turning to the kids)* Kids, come and get ...
10   what in the world?
11   JOHN: *(Turning also to the kids)* Where are your clothes?! *(Pause)*
12   Well, get 'em back on — it's time to eat! *(Turning to DAVE)*
13   They don't have a chance of inheriting the world, do they?
14   DAVE: Not a prayer. *(They exit.)*
15
16
17
18
19
20
21
22
23
24
25
26
27
28
29
30
31
32
33
34
35

By the Book

A sketch on legalism.

Theme: Legalism, pharisaic behavior, judging others, forgiveness

Scripture References: Matthew 12:10-12, Matthew 13:40-43, Matthew 13:47-49, Romans 3:23, 1 Corinthians 4:5

Synopsis: An intern who is just a little overzealous about not letting souls into heaven needs some tutoring on the most important deciding factor.

Cast: Gabriel
Walter

Props: Two clipboards with papers attached, two pens.

Setting: Heaven's gate. A chair (and possibly a desk) should be placed at Center Stage.

1   *(WALTER sits at Center Stage with clipboard in hand. GABRIEL*
2   *strides to Center Stage with a stern look on his face and a clip-*
3   *board in his hand.)*
4   **GABRIEL: Uh … Walter, how's it going?**
5   **WALTER: Great! Couldn't be better, sir! I love this new assignment!**
6   **GABRIEL: Uh, yes. I can tell. You're very enthusiastic. I like that!**
7   **WALTER: Well , who wouldn't be? I mean, of all the angel interns,**
8   **I get put at the gate to handle admissions! What a thrill!**
9   **GABRIEL: Yes, well, I … uh … well, I think we need to talk …**
10   **WALTER: Oh?** *(Pause)* **Am I doing something wrong?**
11   **GABRIEL: Well, yes. I mean … maybe. Well, I think there might**
12   **be a problem …**
13   **WALTER: Oh, no! What happened? It was that Messianic Jew I let**
14   **in a while back, wasn't it? I thought he seemed sincere, but …**
15   **GABRIEL: No, no! He was sincere! A very devout man. You did**
16   **well with him, Walter.**
17   **WALTER:** *(Sighs in relief.)* **Whew! Good!** *(Pause)* **But then, what's**
18   **the problem?**
19   **GABRIEL: Well, Walter, I've been going over the numbers, and**
20   **something is definitely wrong.**
21   **WALTER: Huh?**
22   **GABRIEL: Look at this chart.** *(Shows him the clipboard.)* **Now, this**
23   **line way up here represents admissions before you took over**
24   **your front gate duties two weeks ago.**
25   **WALTER:** *(Looking at chart)* **Uh-huh …**
26   **GABRIEL: And this line way down here represents admissions**
27   **since then …**
28   **WALTER: Yeah?** *(Pause)* **So what's the problem?**
29   **GABRIEL: Well, it seems to me that we should be admitting far**
30   **more people into heaven than we are.** *(Pause)* **So why have the**
31   **numbers been so low lately?**
32   **WALTER: Honestly?**
33   **GABRIEL: Yes, honestly.**
34   **WALTER:** *(Glancing around suspiciously)* **I think it's cable TV!**
35   **GABRIEL: What?**

1   WALTER: Seriously. There are so many awful things …

2   GABRIEL: No, no, no! Cable TV is not the reason!

3   WALTER: It couldn't help!

4   GABRIEL: Listen, Walter. I like your enthusiasm and your energy.

5   I think you'll make a terrific angel one day. But I think you

6   might be a bit too hard on people as they ask to be let in.

7   WALTER: You think so?

8   GABRIEL: Well, let's look at your chart for today, for example.

9   Can we? *(Pointing to table)*

10 WALTER: By all means!

11 GABRIEL: *(Picking up clipboard off table and reading it)* Let's see.

12   *(Pause)* OK. Now here's an example. Mr. Fred Needlemeyer.

13   Admission denied. Reason? Impure thoughts about his ninth-

14   grade English teacher.

15 WALTER: Mrs. Crandall.

16 GABRIEL: Yes, Mrs. Crandall. *(Pause)* Did you ask him if he had

17   asked for forgiveness?

18 WALTER: Well, yes — of course.

19 GABRIEL: And?

20 WALTER: Well, he had for some of the thoughts. But he had a lot

21   of 'em.

22 GABRIEL: I see. *(Pause)* Here's another one. Stefan Carswell.

23   Admission denied. Reason? Stole a car in 1987. Porsche. Light

24   Blue. License number …

25 WALTER: HD35289.

26 GABRIEL: Yes. Did you ask him if he had asked for forgiveness?

27 WALTER: Yes, sir, he had. But I'm not sure he meant it.

28 GABRIEL: Uh-huh. *(Pause)* And how about this one? Samantha

29   Lawrence. Overdue library books?

30 WALTER: She never took them back!

31 GABRIEL: OK, listen. We're going to need to go over this again.

32   There is one criterion for getting through those gates. *(Point-*

33   *ing behind them, then pointing back to a previous page of*

34   *instructions on the clipboard.)* You ask them if they know Jesus

35   Christ as their own personal Lord and Savior. If they have

1 asked him into their hearts, they're in.
2 WALTER: Yes, sir. I remember that part. But the Bible clearly stip-
3 ulates that there is a code of conduct within which we are to
4 live ...
5 GABRIEL: Yes, yes, yes. But the bottom line is also found in the
6 Bible. "Whosoever believeth in me shall not perish, but have
7 everlasting life (John 3:16, author's paraphrase)." That's Jesus
8 talking.
9 WALTER: Yes, sir, I know, but ...
10 GABRIEL: God. The everlasting one. *(Pause)* Your boss!
11 WALTER: *(Pause)* Yes, sir. It's just that I have a hard time letting
12 someone like these people in at the same time as I let Joan of
13 Arc in. Or Stephen the Martyr. Or Paul ...
14 GABRIEL: Did you get a good look at the rap sheet on Paul? If God
15 can overlook all the things in Paul's past, I would think you
16 would be able to as well. Remember, if they have asked Jesus
17 into their hearts, you must let 'em through the pearly gates!
18 WALTER: Yes, sir, I suppose so. But what if they don't deserve it?
19 GABRIEL: Walter, no one deserves it. Read Romans 3:23 again.
20 "For *all* have sinned and fall short of the glory of God." Just
21 because we have sinned doesn't mean that God can't overlook
22 that if we ask him to.
23 WALTER: I guess you're right.
24 GABRIEL: And besides, *(Looking at the clipboard again)* if you
25 denied admission to everyone who worked on the Sabbath,
26 even Jesus wouldn't be able to get past you!
27 WALTER: Really? Wow. I think I've got some work to do.
28 GABRIEL: You think you can find everyone on this list and tell
29 them to revisit the gates? Only this time, just ask the
30 questions on the clipboard.
31 WALTER: I can try.
32 GABRIEL: Good. I hope you can. For all their sakes. *(Looking at the*
33 *clipboard again)* Especially this one. Running an orphanage
34 without a license?
35 WALTER: Oh, my goodness! I remember that lady. She seemed

1   **pretty nice otherwise. Maybe I can still catch her!** *(Runs*
2   *Off-stage.)*
3   **GABRIEL:** *(Pausing as he reads)* **Wait a minute! Walter, you didn't!**
4   **You turned away Mother Teresa?!** *(Runs after him.)*
5
6
7
8
9
10
11
12
13
14
15
16
17
18
19
20
21
22
23
24
25
26
27
28
29
30
31
32
33
34
35

Compassion?

A sketch about Jesus' compassion,
even when he was suffering.

Theme: Compassion

Scripture
References: 2 Kings 4:32-36, Mark 2:3, Ephesians 4:32

Synopsis: As a father works on the family taxes, his son reminds him of Jesus' compassion, even when he was being crucified — then he gives Dad an unexpected chance of his own to be compassionate.

Cast: Dad
Son

Props: Papers, report card.

Setting: The living room. Set a small table and chair at Center Stage.

1   *(DAD sits at a table, which is covered with papers. He is busily*
2   *working on the family's taxes. He is obviously frustrated. His SON*
3   *walks in from Stage Right.)*
4   **DAD: Oh, I hate taxes. IRS doesn't stand for Internal Revenue**
5   **Service. Probably stands for "Income Taxes Really Stink!"**
6   **SON: Hey, Dad! How's it going?**
7   **DAD:** *(Mumbling, then looks up)* **Oh, hey, deduction. I mean, uh ...**
8   *(Snapping his fingers, trying to remember his name)* **Curtis.**
9   **SON: Whatcha doing?**
10   **DAD: Huh?** *(Still working)* **Oh, uh ... taxes.**
11   **SON: Ah!** *(Fidgeting back and forth, stalling)* **So, how's it going?**
12   **DAD: Oh, terrible. I see no way for a refund this year. Unless I**
13   **stretch the truth about the twenty-seven dollars we gave to the**
14   **church this year.**
15   **SON: I see.** *(Still stalling)* **Hey, I was reading in the Bible the other**
16   **day ...**
17   **DAD: Yeah?** *(Doesn't look up, still engrossed in the taxes.)*
18   **SON: Yeah. You know how it's almost April, and Easter is coming ...**
19   **DAD: April 15th, yeah, yeah ...**
20   **SON: Yeah, close. Anyway, I was reading the story of when Jesus**
21   **was on the cross, you know?**
22   **DAD:** *(Mumbling)* **Uh-huh ...**
23   **SON: And you know what he was most concerned about, even**
24   **though he was suffering?**
25   **DAD:** *(Mumbling to himself)* **Charitable contributions.**
26   **SON: Close. He was most concerned about his family. You know,**
27   **who would take care of his mother. He had compassion for**
28   **those who would still be here after his suffering was over.**
29   **DAD:** *(Still not paying attention)* **Compassion. Hey, that's right! We**
30   **sponsored a kid for three weeks last summer through Com-**
31   **passionate Hearts! Where is that receipt?**
32   **SON: Well, I know that you're not in the best mood, what with**
33   **wrestling with Uncle Sam and all, but I just thought I'd men-**
34   **tion how Jesus dealt with stress and stuff. You know, by being**
35   **compassionate toward those he loved.**

1   **DAD:** *(Still distracted and mumbling)* **Uh-huh.** *(Grabs paper.)* **Ah,**
2   **here it is — Compassionate Hearts!**
3   **SON: Well, just wanted to let you know that I think it's great how**
4   **you take care of things like this, Dad.**
5   **DAD: Huh? Oh, yeah. No problem — it's part of my job.**
6   **SON: And I think you're doing a terrific job. Keep it up!** *(Starts to*
7   *walk out, then fakes like he just remembered the report card in his*
8   *hand.)* **Oh yeah, I almost forgot! We got our progress reports**
9   **on Friday. You can just sign it when you get time.** *(Puts the*
10   *report card on the stack of papers and sneaks out.)* **See ya, Dad!**
11   **You're the best!**
12   **DAD: Uh-huh.** *(Shuffling through papers and mumbling)* **OK, now**
13   **where was I? Oh yeah, I was looking for my tax-sheltered**
14   **annuities stuff ... Let's see, two hundred a month into our**
15   **mutual funds, one hundred into our IRA, and a D in Algebra.**
16   *(Pause)* **A** *D* **in Algebra! Curtis, you get back here — you're**
17   **not talking your way out of this one!** *(Storms off to find SON.)*
18
19
20
21
22
23
24
25
26
27
28
29
30
31
32
33
34
35

Details, Details

A sketch about worry.

Theme: Worry

Scripture References: Genesis 7:16, Matthew 6:25-34

Synopsis: When Noah starts to stress about all the animals he has to inventory prior to setting sail, his wife reminds him that God is in control.

Cast: Noah
Noah's Wife

Props: Clipboard with paper, pen.

Sound Effects: Thunder.

Setting: The ark.

1   *(NOAH has a clipboard in hand, and is busily trying to inventory*
2   *all the animals before the rain starts to fall. His WIFE enters.)*
3   **WIFE: Noah? Are you all right?**
4   **NOAH: I haven't seen any koala bears! It's starting to cloud over**
5   **and I haven't seen any koala bears!**
6   **WIFE: Calm down, dear. I'll help you look. Now, what do they look**
7   **like?**
8   **NOAH: Well, they ... I think they're ...** *(Shouting)* **Doggone it! It's**
9   **about to rain and I don't even know what a koala bear**
10   **looks like!**
11   **WIFE: Noah, I'm sure we'll find one before ...**
12   **NOAH:** *One* **isn't going to do me any good! See, it takes two to**
13   **make a pair, and I don't know what one looks like, let alone**
14   **how to tell the koala she from the koala he!**
15   **WIFE: Now Noah, I think you're making a mountain out of a**
16   **molehill.**
17   **NOAH:** *(Pausing, bolt upright)* **Oh, no! I forgot the dirt for the moles!**
18   **They'll be digging holes through the bottom of the boat!**
19   **WIFE: Oye! You can't do this to yourself. You're going to have a**
20   **breakdown.**
21   **NOAH: Nope, don't have time! Who else is going to make sure that**
22   **the species continue? God left this responsibility to me!** *Me!*
23   **How am I ever going to figure out what is what and who's who?**
24   **WIFE: What are you talking about?**
25   **NOAH: I'm talking animals! I'm the wrong man for this job!**
26   **WIFE: Of course you're the right man. Why else would God have**
27   **picked you?**
28   **NOAH:** *(Looking around suspiciously)* **No other reason! Why? Have**
29   **you heard something?**
30   **WIFE: Noah, what has gotten into you?**
31   **NOAH: Oh, all right!** *(Looking around to make sure no one is*
32   *listening)* **All right. I think that ... Oh!**
33   **WIFE: What is it?**
34   **NOAH: Oh, I think God may be trying to punish me.** *That's* **why he**
35   **picked me.**

1   WIFE: Noah! Don't be ridiculous!

2   NOAH: No, I'm serious. You remember why we don't have a cat?

3   WIFE: You have allergies, right?

4   NOAH: Oh, that's just what I told Shem so he would stop bugging

5   me! We don't have a cat because I hate cats!

6   WIFE: So? Who doesn't hate cats?

7   NOAH: No! I really hate cats! I ... I ... I'm no good with animals.

8   My mom used to stuff my clothes full of oats just to get the

9   donkey to come close enough for me to pet.

10   WIFE: Oh, Noah! You're exaggerating!

11   NOAH: No, I'm not! I think God picked me for this job because he

12   knows how badly I'm going to do, and everyone will laugh

13   at me!

14   WIFE: Oh, Noah. Only the really good swimmers will laugh for

15   very long. *(Pause)* And besides, I think you're missing the boat

16   on what God expects from you.

17   NOAH: That was really bad. But what do you mean?

18   WIFE: Well, all this categorizing, for instance. Do you really think

19   it's necessary?

20   NOAH: Well, of course it's necessary! How else will we have two of

21   everything?

22   WIFE: Well, now, you know how God told you exactly how big to

23   make the ark?

24   NOAH: Yes?

25   WIFE: And how wide and how tall and how many levels and how

26   many inches to leave for the ceiling and what to build it out of

27   and where to put the door ...

28   NOAH: Yes, yes, of course. What's your point?

29   WIFE: Well, I was wondering where you got your list for the animals.

30   NOAH: Well, I made it up from what I knew. I have to keep adding

31   to it as new animals show up.

32   WIFE: Ah! So God didn't give you a specific list?

33   NOAH: No, he just told me to get two of everything ...

34   WIFE: And the animals keep showing up? Noah, how long ago did

35   God tell you to get the animals together?

1 NOAH: It's been nearly a week. And the rain is supposed to come
2   any minute!
3 WIFE: Don't you see?
4 NOAH: See what?
5 WIFE: Noah, God is going to make sure that all the animals get
6   here. He knows that it's beyond human capability to get all
7   these things together in just one week without his help. That's
8   why new animals keep showing up.
9 NOAH: Really? So you think I should trust that God is going to
10   make sure that all the animals find their way here?
11 WIFE: I think that God just wants you to be obedient to what he
12   tells you and he'll take care of details. *(Pause)* And de heads,
13   and de legs ...
14 NOAH: Eight months of those kinds of jokes and I'll jump over-
15   board. *(Pause as he looks at something crossing the stage in front*
16   *of him.)* Hey! Aren't those ...
17 WIFE: Koala bears? Well, it looks to me like you've got quite a
18   group assembled already. *(Thunder is heard in the background.)*
19   And just in time, too!
20 NOAH: Wow! I guess you're right! *(Yelling Off-stage)* Shem! Ham!
21   Japheth! Grab those camels and flamingoes and get 'em
22   inside! And don't goof off! *(Pause)* Or I'll ground you!
23 WIFE: Very funny. Now do you feel more at ease with everything?
24 NOAH: Actually, I do. Well, as at ease as I could be, knowing that
25   we're about to spend the next eight months with 45,000
26   screeching birds, snakes, and mammals. Thanks, dear.
27 WIFE: That's why I'm here. We'd better get on board. It's starting
28   to sprinkle.
29 NOAH: OK, let's go! *(They begin to exit, with NOAH looking over his*
30   *list again.)* There's still one thing that bothers me, though ...
31 WIFE: What's that?
32 NOAH: I only remember seeing one unicorn ...
33
34
35

Disorder in the Court!

*A sketch that looks at what
turning the other cheek really means.*

Theme: Turning the other cheek, Christian character,
loving your enemies

**Scripture
References:**   Matthew 5:35-43; Luke 6:26-27;
Romans 12:17, 20; 1 Peter 3:9

Synopsis: A scam artist who fakes injuries following a
minor traffic accident is stunned when he is
offered twice what he was asking for in an out-
of-court settlement.

Cast: Bailiff
Judge
Mr. Mulrooney (plaintiff)
Plaintiff Attorney
Ms. Davis (defendant)
Defense Attorney

Props: Gavel for the Judge.

Setting: A courtroom. There is a table and chair at Center Stage for the Judge, a table and two chairs
for Mr. Mulrooney and the Plaintiff Attorney
to one side of the Judge, and a table and two
chairs on the other side for Ms. Davis and the
Defense Attorney.

1   *(MS. DAVIS, the defendant, is seated on one side with the*
2   *DEFENSE ATTORNEY. MR. MULROONEY, the plaintiff with many*
3   *obviously questionable injuries, is seated on the other side with the*
4   *PLAINTIFF ATTORNEY. BAILIFF stands by the entrance.)*
5   **BAILIFF: All rise! The honorable Judge Smith is now entering the**
6   **courtroom.** *(Everyone stands as JUDGE enters.)*
7   **JUDGE: Be seated.** *(All sit.)* **First case is Mulrooney vs. Davis.**
8   **Disposition, Bailiff?**
9   **BAILIFF: Yes, sir. It seems that Ms. Davis here bumped into Mr.**
10   **Mulrooney at a stoplight. There was no damage to either**
11   **vehicle, but Mr. Mulrooney has come down with a variety of**
12   **maladies he claims are resulting from the accident.**
13   **MR. MULROONEY:** *(Faking like he is in pain)* **Oooohhhhhhh!**
14   **PLAINTIFF ATTORNEY: I object!**
15   **JUDGE: To what?**
16   **PLAINTIFF ATTORNEY: To the implication.**
17   **JUDGE: What implication?**
18   **PLAINTIFF ATTORNEY:** *(Pause)* **OK, I may have jumped the gun**
19   **a bit there. Sorry.**
20   **JUDGE: Oh, brother. Proceed with your argument, Mr. Attorney.**
21   **PLAINTIFF ATTORNEY: Thank you, Your Honor. Now, as was**
22   **stated, the defendant recklessly and without concern for the**
23   **welfare of my client, slammed into the rear of my client's**
24   **vehicle, causing his head to snap back and nearly damage his**
25   **spinal cord. The resulting whiplash has left my client as you**
26   **see him here — a broken man. We are seeking damages in the**
27   **amount of five thousand dollars.**
28   **MR. MULROONEY: Ohhh …**
29   **JUDGE: Mr. Mulrooney, I'm going to have to ask you to suffer**
30   **more quietly. Defense?**
31   **DEFENSE ATTORNEY: Your honor, before I begin, may I just say**
32   **that I feel the injuries in question could not have been caused**
33   **by the aforementioned accident? My client simply didn't have**
34   **her foot on the brake as hard as she should have and the two**
35   **cars touched bumpers.**

1   **PLAINTIFF ATTORNEY: I object!**

2   **MR. MULROONEY: Ohhh …**

3   **JUDGE: Yes?**

4   **PLAINTIFF ATTORNEY: Is my esteemed colleague now into prac-**

5   **ticing medicine?**

6   **DEFENSE ATTORNEY: As much as you are into practicing law,**

7   **Clark! By the way, how's the Scamway business going?**

8   **JUDGE:** *(Pounds gavel.)* **Order! I will not have the two of you at**

9   **each other's throats today! And by the way, overruled.**

10   **DEFENSE ATTORNEY: Thank you, Your Honor. As I was saying,**

11   **even though my client could not have caused the plaintiff's**

12   **injuries, …** *(Pause)* **and it pains me to …**

13   **JUDGE:** *(After a pause)* **Yes?**

14   **DEFENSE ATTORNEY:** *(Pause)* **Against my legal counsel, and**

15   **everything that is decent and fair, my client wishes to settle**

16   **with the plaintiff.**

17   **PLAINTIFF ATTORNEY: I object!**

18   **JUDGE: To what now?**

19   **PLAINTIFF ATTORNEY: This is obviously a ploy to give my client**

20   **less than he deserves.**

21   **DEFENSE ATTORNEY: On the contrary. My client has agreed to**

22   **give your client twice what you are asking.**

23   **MR. MULROONEY: Ohhh?**

24   **PLAINTIFF ATTORNEY: Excuse me?**

25   **JUDGE: Is this true, Ms. Davis?**

26   **MS. DAVIS: Yes, Your Honor.**

27   **JUDGE: May I ask why?**

28   **MS. DAVIS: Well, I did take my foot off the brake, and my car did**

29   **touch his bumper. We wouldn't be here if it wasn't for that.**

30   **DEFENSE ATTORNEY: Your Honor, I object!**

31   **JUDGE: You can't object. That's your client!**

32   **DEFENSE ATTORNEY: Yes, Your Honor, I know, but this just isn't**

33   **right. That freeloader over there is obviously faking. This is a**

34   **no-lose case!**

35   **PLAINTIFF ATTORNEY: I object too, Your Honor!**

1   JUDGE: Why does that not surprise me?
2   MR. MULROONEY: Oooohhh!
3   PLAINTIFF ATTORNEY: *(To MR. MULROONEY)* Oh, shut up.
4   MR. MULROONEY: But you said I should act like …
5   PLAINTIFF ATTORNEY: As I was saying, we've come here to
6   argue a case. What's the fun in quitting before we start?
7   JUDGE: Overruled … the both of you. We can't have a trial if the
8   defendant wants to settle. But I must ask for a little elabora-
9   tion on the defendant's part, if you don't mind.
10 MS. DAVIS: Well, I just don't feel that fighting it is what Jesus
11   would've done.
12 DEFENSE ATTORNEY: Why not?
13 MS. DAVIS: Well, I was reading in the Bible where if a man asks
14   you to walk a mile with him, you should go two. It didn't say
15   anything about arguing with him about the first mile.
16 DEFENSE ATTORNEY: Did it say anything about a countersuit
17   for fraud?
18 JUDGE: I object! *(Pause as all look at him)* I mean, order in the
19   court! *(Pause)* Well, Ms. Davis, you have the right to settle if
20   you so wish …
21 MR. MULROONEY: Wait a minute. What if I decide I don't want
22   your money?
23 PLAINTIFF ATTORNEY: Sit down! *(To JUDGE)* Your Honor, my
24   client is obviously delirious from his medication …
25 MR. MULROONEY: I'm not even on any medication, and you
26   know it. *(To MS. DAVIS)* I'd like to know more about why you
27   want to settle. Could we go out and talk about this over say …
28   lunch? *(He walks over to MS. DAVIS and they begin walking*
29   *out.)*
30 MS. DAVIS: Sure. You know, our pastor is talking on this very sub-
31   ject this Sunday …
32 MR. MULROONEY: Really? I haven't been to church in a while …
33   *(MR. MULROONEY and MS. DAVIS exit, talking.)*
34 BOTH ATTORNEYS: *(Together)* **I object!**
35 JUDGE: Overruled! Case dismissed! *(Pause as ATTORNEYS rise to*

1   *leave. To ATTORNEYS)* **Not so fast, you two! I have some real**
2   **questions about the integrity of this case. I'd like to see both of**
3   **you in my chambers immediately.** *(JUDGE and BAILIFF exit.)*
4 **DEFENSE ATTORNEY: You know, I really don't think we get**
5   **enough exercise. How'd you like to join me in running a mile?**
6 **PLAINTIFF ATTORNEY: I know … how about two?** *(They exit,*
7   *running.)*
8
9
10
11
12
13
14
15
16
17
18
19
20
21
22
23
24
25
26
27
28
29
30
31
32
33
34
35

Do We Have Any Visitors?

A sketch about accepting newcomers to the church.

Theme: Judging others, accepting change and others

Scripture References: Romans 12:13, 1 Timothy 3:2, Matthew 7:1

Synopsis: A church member who inwardly complains about visitors is brought up short by who the Visitor turns out to be. The characters on the stage say nothing. Their thoughts are read by Off-stage voices as they pantomime On-stage.

Cast: *On-stage pantomimers:*
Member (male or female)
Visitor (male)

Off-stage voices:
Pastor's voice
Member's voice
Visitor's voice

Props: Hymnals.

Setting: A church sanctuary. Set up two chairs (or small pews) at an inward-facing angle (inverted V) so that the two characters face each other.

1   *(MEMBER and VISITOR should go up onto the platform during*
2   *the last half of the song that precedes the sketch. Hymnals in hand,*
3   *they finish the song with the congregation, and when it ends, they*
4   *sit down at the same time as the congregation. If the congregation*
5   *is sitting during that song, they should remain standing.)*
6   **PASTOR'S VOICE: You may be seated.** *(They sit.)*
7   **MEMBER'S VOICE: Finally. They make us stand for way too**
8   **many songs. You'd think this was a Catholic church — up,**
9   **down, up, down …**
10 **VISITOR'S VOICE: This seems like a nice enough little church.**
11   **They certainly sing their hearts out. I'm glad I got the chance**
12   **to visit.** *(The Member and the Visitor make eye contact and smile*
13   *at each other sincerely during a pause.)*
14 **MEMBER'S VOICE: I wonder who that is. I've never seen him**
15   **here before.** *(Pause)* **It sure seems like we've had a lot more**
16   **visitors recently.** *(Deep sigh)* **I mean, I guess that's OK and**
17   **everything, but … I just don't see why they have to visit** *our*
18   **church.** *(They make eye contact again and smile.)*
19 **VISITOR'S VOICE: Yes, I could really get to like it here. It's warm,**
20   **sincere … and inviting.**
21 **MEMBER'S VOICE: Wait, that's not what I mean. All I'm saying**
22   **is that if we get too many visitors, it won't be our church any-**
23   **more. We're not big enough to have visitors. Visitors throw off**
24   **our whole balance. Besides, what's his deal? Why this church?**
25   **He probably has some agenda or something …**
26 **VISITOR'S VOICE: I think I could really work well in a church**
27   **like this.**
28 **MEMBER'S VOICE: I suppose the Pastor's going to make us all**
29   **stand up and shake hands with everyone, and I'll end up**
30   **greeting the … alien. Ooooh, that makes me so uncomfort-**
31   **able! I don't know anything about him, and I'll have to think**
32   **of something to say, shake his hand, introduce myself … Those**
33   **things aren't on my top ten list of favorite things to do. I come**
34   **to church to relax and worship — not to learn how to be an**
35   **ambassador of good will. I can be friendly enough, but … I**

1   just hope he doesn't make us stand ...

2   VISITOR'S VOICE: Everyone has been friendly so far — that's a

3   good sign.

4   MEMBER'S VOICE: Look, I've been a member here for years. It's

5   not fair that some visitor shows up on a Sunday and then

6   starts coming on a regular basis. What if he likes it here and

7   then wants to become a member? What if he gets some kind

8   of committee position or whatever and wants to change some-

9   thing that doesn't need to be changed? That's not fair! I've

10   been here a long time, and I like things the way they are.

11   Listen to me — I sound awful! Oh, well ... it's not like anyone

12   can hear what I'm thinking ...

13   VISITOR'S VOICE: I hope that somebody notices that I'm here

14   this morning. That's really why I came ...

15   MEMBER'S VOICE: Besides, we don't know anything about

16   visitors. I mean, this guy could be some fugitive or something.

17   Wouldn't *that* be great. The papers would get hold of the fact

18   that a convicted criminal spent his last Sunday morning as a

19   free man at our church. We'd be a laughingstock. Or what if

20   he's really not a Christian at all? Maybe he's just spending the

21   Sunday recruiting for his own cult or something. After all, he

22   seems awfully friendly ...

23   PASTOR'S VOICE: At this time I'd like to recognize anyone who

24   may be visiting us for the first time this morning. Do we have

25   any visitors?

26   MEMBER'S VOICE: Oh boy, here we go. Just once I'd like to sit

27   here and enjoy the service as a church full of regular members.

28   Why can't people visit the megachurches and leave us alone?

29   PASTOR'S VOICE: I believe I recognize at least one. This is a spe-

30   cial guest of mine whom I hope you'll find the time to meet.

31   Would you stand, please? *(VISITOR stands and smiles, waving*

32   *nicely to the congregation.)* This is a good friend of mine. He's

33   been here before, and I hope he'll be a regular from now on

34   ... Jesus Christ, the Son of God. *(MEMBER shrinks down a lit-*

35   *tle in his seat and smiles hypocritically at VISITOR as he sits*

1   *down. There is a pause.)*
2   **MEMBER'S VOICE: You know, on second thought, a church needs**
3   **visitors every now and then. I mean, after all, it *is* a church ...**
4
5
6
7
8
9
10
11
12
13
14
15
16
17
18
19
20
21
22
23
24
25
26
27
28
29
30
31
32
33
34
35

Don't Worry, Be Happy?

A sketch that examines the practicalities
of joyfully living the Christian life.

Theme: Happiness, faith, hypocrisy

Scripture References: Matthew 21:30-32, Mark 9:50, Philippians 4:4

Synopsis: A guy shares numerous personal problems with his coworker, who tells him not to worry. Then the coworker encounters a problem of his own. Joyfully living the Christian life isn't *that* difficult … or is it?

Cast: Allen
Bill
Carol

Props: None.

Setting: The employee lounge at work. Place a table at Center Stage (the "break table").

1   *(BILL sits at a break table with his head in his hands as ALLEN,*
2   *a coworker, comes onto the scene, whistling a happy tune.)*
3   **ALLEN: Hey, bud! It's a beautiful morning, isn't it?**
4   **BILL:** *(Unsmiling and sarcastic)* **Yeah. Gorgeous.**
5   **ALLEN: Just a guess. Unhappy, right?**
6   **BILL: Is it obvious?**
7   **ALLEN: Slightly. What seems to be the trouble?**
8   **BILL: Well, I just heard through the grapevine that there are going**
9   **to be more layoffs. And I'm low on the seniority ladder.**
10   **ALLEN: That's too bad.**
11   **BILL: And Linda's due in three months.**
12   **ALLEN: That** *is* **tough.**
13   **BILL: And our savings are pretty much gone already, from when**
14   **the tornado wiped us out last summer.**
15   **ALLEN: Another tough break.**
16   **BILL: My life seems so hopeless, you know?**
17   **ALLEN:** *(Sitting down)* **I know it may seem bad, but don't get dis-**
18   **couraged, Bill.**
19   **BILL: That's easy for you to say. What do I have to encourage me?**
20   **ALLEN: Well, Bill, you're a Christian, right?**
21   **BILL: Well, yes. But that doesn't mean I don't have problems.**
22   **ALLEN: No, maybe not. But the Bible says not to worry about 'em.**
23   **BILL: Right. That's easy enough when the problems are small,**
24   **but …**
25   **ALLEN: In Philippians it says, "Don't fret or worry. Instead of**
26   **worrying, pray (Philippians 4:6, TM)." Then you will be just as**
27   **happy when things are rough as you would be if things**
28   **were perfect.**
29   **BILL: Well, I don't know about that …**
30   **ALLEN: What could it hurt, though? Are you happier worrying**
31   **about things more?**
32   **BILL: Certainly not! But what kind of person would I be if I**
33   **didn't worry about my family?**
34   **ALLEN: Look. You're doing all you can do, right?**
35   **BILL: Right …**

1   ALLEN: Adding worry to the list will just take energy away from
2   the problems you need to deal with. Let go of the worry. You
3   can overcome anything by giving it over to God.
4   BILL: You know, I'll bet you're right. I'm going to try that right
5   away.
6   ALLEN: That's the spirit. I know you'll be happier.
7   BILL: I'm happier already … *(CAROL comes in from Off-stage.)*
8   CAROL: Hey, you guys! Did you see the size of the hail outside? It
9   must be baseball-sized!
10   ALLEN: OH NO, NOT MY BRAND NEW BMW! *(Runs outside,*
11   *still yelling.)* I have a $250 deductible!
12   BILL: *(To audience)* Looks like somebody may need to read Philip-
13   pians again …
14
15
16
17
18
19
20
21
22
23
24
25
26
27
28
29
30
31
32
33
34
35

Easy Come, Easy Go

A sketch on the fleeting nature of earthly treasure.

Theme: Earthly treasures, fame, wealth

Scripture References: Luke 6:26, Revelation 18:11-19, Matthew 6:19

Synopsis: The winner of a sand-sculpting contest has spent hours recreating the Sistine Chapel — only to have it washed away by the tide.

Cast: Reporter
Winner
Camera Man (Off-stage voice)
Well-wisher extras (optional number)

Props: Microphone.

Sound Effects: Sea noises (optional).

Setting: A beach.

1   *(The scene opens with the REPORTER talking as the WINNER*
2   *shakes hands with WELL-WISHERS. If possible, sea noises may*
3   *be playing in the background.)*
4   **REPORTER: Sandy Madras here, covering the seventeenth**
5   **annual Sand-Sculpting World Championships, and it appears**
6   **that we have a winner! I'm going to try to get an interview**
7   **with this year's champion … if we can get through to him here**
8   **… here we go! Excuse me, sir?** *(Pause as last of the crowd*
9   *shakes his hand)* **Sir? Sandy Madras here with Global News**
10   **Network. Can we have a word with you?**
11   **WINNER:** *(Noticing the cameras)* **Uh … what? Oh! Sure!**
12   **REPORTER: What is your name?**
13   **WINNER: Huh?** *(Pause)* **Say, are we on TV?**
14   **REPORTER: Yes sir. Can you tell us your name?**
15   **WINNER: Wow! Uh..what? Oh, yes. I'm Trevor Braxton. From**
16   **Normal, Illinois. Hi Mom! They will see this in Illinois,**
17   **won't they?**
18   **REPORTER: Uh, yes, sir — unless, of course, we get preempted by**
19   **something more important. Like rain, for example.** *(WINNER*
20   *pays no attention after the "yes, sir" — instead, he is waving furi-*
21   *ously at the camera.)* **Anyway, Mr. Braxton, congratulations on**
22   **your sculpting victory! You must be very proud!**
23   **WINNER: Thanks! Thanks a lot! I really am. I've been working my**
24   **whole life for this moment!**
25   **REPORTER: You've been sand sculpting your whole life? Growing**
26   **up in Illinois?**
27   **WINNER: Yup! Dad put a huge sandbox in the back yard, and the**
28   **rest is history!**
29   **REPORTER: Wow. He built you a sandbox just so you could**
30   **practice sculpting?**
31   **WINNER: Yep! Well, not just for me — we did have a lot of cats.**
32   *(Waves again to the camera.)* **Hi, Dad!**
33   **REPORTER: I see. So tell me about your sculpture.**
34   **WINNER: Well, as you can see, it's an exact replica of the Sistine**
35   **Chapel in Vatican City.** *(Leaning down as if to point inside the*

1   *invisible structure)* **As you can see here, I used watercolors to**
2   **reproduce Michelangelo's ceiling masterpieces on the inside.**
3 **REPORTER: Wow! This is truly amazing!**
4 **WINNER: Thanks!**
5 **REPORTER: And exactly how long have you been working on this?**
6 **WINNER: It was nineteen weeks last Thursday.**
7 **REPORTER: Oh, my! And do you mind if I ask what motivated you**
8   **to spend more than four months on a sand sculpture?**
9 **WINNER: Certainly. You see, when I heard about this contest, I**
10   **knew this was my chance to shine! I knew that with my**
11   **ability I could be famous, and sure enough, here I am on tele-**
12   **vision!** *(Waves again to the camera.)*
13 **REPORTER: Yes, I see. But you obviously went weeks beyond the**
14   **time most of the contestants did. Why?**
15 **WINNER: Well, Sandy ... can I call you Sandy?**
16 **REPORTER: Uh ... yeah, I guess ...**
17 **WINNER: Well, Sandy, ever since my brother failed to make it as a**
18   **juggling clown, I vowed that someday I would bring honor to**
19   **the family name once again. That I would be famous one day.**
20   **And that day has finally arrived.**
21 **REPORTER: Your brother was a juggling clown?**
22 **WINNER: Yep. Well, he was until the knife accident. Had to give it**
23   **up after that. Too tough to juggle with seven fingers.**
24 **REPORTER:Yes, well ... what do you plan to do with the two-**
25   **hundred-dollar prize?**
26 **WINNER: Well, since I haven't worked for the last five months, I**
27   **think the first thing I'll do is buy groceries.**
28 **REPORTER: Uh-huh.**
29 **WINNER: But as soon as everyone finds out about this, I'll be so**
30   **famous the money will just roll in.**
31 **REPORTER: Really? From sand sculpting?**
32 **WINNER: You bet! As soon as the rest of the networks get here, I'll**
33   **be on my way to fame and fortune!**
34 **REPORTER: Well, good luck, Trevor.** *(Turns back to the camera.)*
35   **That's Trevor Braxton from Normal, Illinois, this year's**

1   sculpting champion. Well, that's it from Hermosa Beach and
2   the seventeenth annual Sand-Sculpting Competition. I'm
3   Sandy Madras for GNN.
4   CAMERA MAN: *(Off-stage)* Cut! That's a wrap!
5   WINNER: What? That's it?
6   REPORTER: Are you kidding? We gotta get wrapped up and out
7   of here before the tide gets our equipment all wet.
8   WINNER: Yeah, but what about my fame?
9   REPORTER: You're done. See ya! *(REPORTER exits.)*
10 WINNER: But … where are the other networks? What do I do
11 now? Wait a minute! *(Pause)* Did you say tide? *(Pause)* OH,
12 NO! Stop! *(Pantomimes getting to a higher place while the tide*
13 *wipes out his creation. From his higher vantage point, he should*
14 *step down into the "surf" and look hopelessly at what the tide is*
15 *doing to his sculpture. After a few seconds, he shrugs his shoul-*
16 *ders and puts his hands in his pockets.)*
17 WINNER: Well … I can always build another one, I guess … *(He*
18 *should pause for a few seconds before walking slowly away, look-*
19 *ing back over his shoulder at his ruined masterpiece, and also for*
20 *the reporter who is already gone. He exits slowly.)*
21
22
23
24
25
26
27
28
29
30
31
32
33
34
35

Extra Innings

A sketch concerning eternity.

Theme: Eternity

**Scripture
References:** Matthew 16:26, 2 Corinthians 5:5

Synopsis: A ball game that seems to go on and on serves as a metaphor for eternity.

Cast: Announcer
Player 1
Player 2

Props: Magazine, baseball caps (optional).

Setting: The bench, during the ninth inning of a very important game. Line up a row of chairs or use a small church pew for the bench.

1   *(Two PLAYERS sit on the bench, discussing the possible outcome*

2   *of the game that is being played.)*

3   ANNOUNCER: *(In the background)* **Well, here we go! The** *(Insert*

4   *church team's name)* **and Joe's Bar have struggled to a seven-**

5   **seven tie as we head to the bottom of the twenty-first inning.**

6   **Leading off will be** *(Insert member's name.)* ...

7   PLAYER 1: Some game, huh?

8   PLAYER 2: *(Distracted, even thumbing through a magazine)* **Huh?**

9   **Oh, yeah! It is, isn't it?**

10   PLAYER 1: Yeah. All we need is one run and the ball game is over!

11   The championship will be ours!

12   PLAYER 2: Well, that's a nice thought. But I have a hunch that the

13   ball game will never be over.

14   PLAYER 1: What?

15   ANNOUNCER: There's a line drive to left center, a clean base hit!

16   The *(Insert church team's name)* have the winning run on first

17   with nobody out!

18   PLAYER 1: Hey, all right!

19   PLAYER 2: I said this ballgame will never end.

20   PLAYER 1: Well, it seemed like it for a while, but I think we can

21   still score.

22   PLAYER 2: Scoring is not really all that important. I mean, the ball

23   game goes on. And, for the record, we won't score.

24   PLAYER 1: How do you know? And scoring is what it's all about

25   — one run and we win the game!

26   PLAYER 2: I know. And that's not really what I'm talking about.

27   ANNOUNCER: *(Insert member's name)* at the plate ... here's the

28   delivery ... and there's another screamer down the left field

29   line! The left fielder races over to cut it off and fires it to third

30   to hold runners at first and second with nobody out!

31   PLAYER 1: Nice shot! This is a great set-up. I tell you, this game is

32   almost over!

33   PLAYER 2: No, it's not. It will go on forever!

34   PLAYER 1: What are you talking about?

35   PLAYER 2: Look. We all look at things in such finite terms. If I can

1   just make it till Friday. If I can just work ten more years, then
2   I can retire. If I can keep eating broccoli until next Thursday,
3   I'll be able to wear my old jeans again...
4   PLAYER 1: *(Ignoring PLAYER 2 completely)* If we could just get one
5   more hit!
6   PLAYER 2: Exactly. But it just isn't going to happen.
7   PLAYER 1: Listen. I think you have a very negative attitude.
8   PLAYER 2: On the contrary. I'm very positive. That this game will
9   not end.
10   PLAYER 1: How can you say that? We have runners on first and
11   second with nobody out! We just need one run. How can you
12   say this game isn't about to end?
13   PLAYER 2: Number one, it's our church. Number two, that isn't
14   the way God set things up. He didn't say, "Let's go nine
15   innings and whoever scores the most, wins." Abner Doubleday
16   did that.
17   PLAYER 1: So what are you saying ... that no matter what we do,
18   the game never ends?
19   PLAYER 2: Now you're getting it.
20   ANNOUNCER: *(Insert member's name)* steps up ... here's the pitch
21   ... *(Member's name)* rifles one to the hole at short, the short-
22   stop dives and knocks the ball down, but he won't have a play
23   anywhere, and the *(Church team's name)* have the bases loaded
24   and nobody out for their clean-up hitter *(Insert member's*
25   *name)*!
26   PLAYER 1: Ha! Nice hustle, *(Insert member's name)*! *(Turning to*
27   *PLAYER 2)* Now what do you say, smarty-pants — bases
28   loaded, nobody out, *(Insert member's name)* coming up ...
29   PLAYER 2: It's not going to happen.
30   PLAYER 1: *(To the field)* Come on, *(Insert member's name)*!
31   PLAYER 2: Don't bet on it. The game will never end.
32   PLAYER 1: Listen, if we don't win this game, right here, right now,
33   I'll ... I'll ...
34   PLAYER 2: Hold it. Don't make promises you may have to keep.
35   PLAYER 1: How do you know it won't end right here? Everything

1   points to this game being over.

2   PLAYER 2: Have you heard of eternity?

3   PLAYER 1: The perfume?

4   PLAYER 2: No! I'm talking forever.

5   PLAYER 1: It sure seems like it.

6   PLAYER 2: Ha, ha. Have you ever thought about what forever

7   means? I mean, *really* thought about it?

8   PLAYER 1: Hmmm. I guess not. It's kinda hard to imagine.

9   PLAYER 2: Like it's hard to imagine this game going on?

10   PLAYER 1: Well, harder than that, actually, but ... sort of.

11   PLAYER 2: Well, it will. And the more often we realize that, the

12   better we'll be able to picture going on forever.

13   PLAYER 1: I can't picture going on like this forever. I don't exactly

14   want to.

15   PLAYER 2: See, that's the thing. It won't be like this. In heaven,

16   you actually win, even though it never ends.

17   PLAYER 1: But we're going to win this game! It's too perfect!

18   PLAYER 2: I don't think so, Tim. Watch.

19   ANNOUNCER: *(Insert member's name)* swings and scorches a liner

20   right at the third baseman. He runs to the bag to double the

21   man off third and fires to first for a triple play! Oh my, what

22   a lost opportunity! We'll go to the twenty-second inning, still

23   tied, seven all.

24   PLAYER 1: I don't believe it!

25   PLAYER 2: I told you. The game will never end.

26   PLAYER 1: I think I get it now. *(Pause)* If we start thinking in

27   terms of forever, things don't seem so pointless, and discour-

28   agement will seem less eternal!

29   PLAYER 2: You're getting there. Some things will pass away. But

30   we won't. So we might as well start acting like we know that

31   by living tomorrow today.

32   PLAYER 1: OK. But you gotta tell me, how did you know what was

33   going to happen in that game?

34   PLAYER 2: Oh, that's easy. I used to play for the Angels ...

35

Give Us This Day Our Daily ... Guacamole?

A sketch on finding fulfillment.

Theme: Fulfillment, the Bread of Life

Scripture Reference: John 6:35

Synopsis: A seeker climbs a mountaintop to find a guru's answer to the meaning of life, but he's had access to the real answer all along.

Cast: Guru
Climber

Props: Towel, index card, large Bible.

Setting: A mountaintop.

1   *(A wise GURU-type guy is sitting in the lotus position in a medi-*
2   *tative state on the floor Center Stage, possibly wrapped in a*
3   *towel. A CLIMBER [Pantomiming climbing] reaches the summit*
4   *to ask for wisdom on the meaning of life.)*
5   **CLIMBER:** *(Panting)* **You ARE here!** *(Panting)* **I always thought**
6   **that finding wise old men on the mountaintops was just a**
7   **myth!**
8   **GURU: Welcome. But for the record, I'm not** *that* **old.**
9   **CLIMBER: Oh, sorry. No offense.**
10   **GURU: None taken, oh less-than-wise one.** *(Pause)* **I've been**
11   **expecting you.**
12   **CLIMBER: You have?**
13   **GURU: Of course. Many have climbed this mountain risking their**
14   **very existence, seeking the knowledge that I am about to share**
15   **with you.**
16   **CLIMBER: They have? Oh, of course they have. And you'll share**
17   **it with me?**
18   **GURU: Of course. Because of the number of requests I receive, I've**
19   **taken the liberty of copying index cards with the information.**
20   **It saves a lot of time.** *(Hands him the card.)*
21   **CLIMBER: Wow!** *(Taking the card)* **You** *are* **wise. Thank you!**
22   **GURU: Good day.**
23   **CLIMBER:** *(Turning and reading the card as he turns to go)* **Hey ...**
24   **this isn't what I was looking for!**
25   **GURU: Excuse me?**
26   **CLIMBER: This is a recipe for guacamole.**
27   **GURU: So what's the problem? Do I use too much garlic for**
28   **your taste?**
29   **CLIMBER: No, no! I'm sure it's quite good.**
30   **GURU: It's the best. Why else would people like yourself climb this**
31   **mountain to get it?**
32   **CLIMBER: I didn't climb this mountain to get a recipe for**
33   **guacamole!**
34   **GURU: Oh?**
35   **CLIMBER: No! I'm searching for the meaning of life!**

1 GURU: Really? That's odd. Haven't had that request since the
2   early seventies ...
3 CLIMBER: *(Pause)* Well?
4 GURU: Oh. Yes, of course. *(Pause)* Why on earth would you climb
5   a mountain to ask something so elementary as that?
6 CLIMBER: What? You just told me that you get lots of people up
7   here looking for the recipe for guacamole!
8 GURU: No, no, no. I said I get lots of people up here looking for *my*
9   recipe for guacamole! *Big* difference.
10 CLIMBER: What?
11 GURU: It's incredible guacamole.
12 CLIMBER: I'm sure it is! But I'm not looking for the recipe for
13   guacamole.
14 GURU: Oh, yes! You're a rather slow chap who's looking for the
15   meaning of life.
16 CLIMBER: Yes! *(Pause)* What? Rather slow?!
17 GURU: My point exactly. Listen, if you want to know the meaning
18   of life ... *(Pause as he retrieves a rather large book)* The answer
19   lies in here ...
20 CLIMBER: Ah! Now we're getting somewhere! Is that a book that
21   has been handed down from generation to generation of wise
22   men in your family?
23 GURU: Not exactly. It's a Bible.
24 CLIMBER: A Bible?
25 GURU: Yes. New International Version. Got it from a delightful
26   young Gideon in trade for the guacamole recipe ...
27 CLIMBER: *(Pause)* You mean the answer to the meaning of life is
28   in *there*?
29 GURU: Yes it is, Einstein.
30 CLIMBER: But I have one of those at *home*.
31 GURU: You ought to try opening it. Could have saved you a trip.
32 CLIMBER: But I *do* read it! All the time!
33 GURU: Well, then you should be familiar with John 6:35. *(Reading,*
34   *or from memory)* Then Jesus declared, "I am the bread of life.
35   He who comes to me will never go hungry, and he who believes

1   in me will never be thirsty."

2   CLIMBER: I know that verse!

3   GURU: Then what are you doing here?

4   CLIMBER: *(Pause)* But it can't be that simple!

5   GURU: I guess it can't if you don't want it to be. But if you're look-
6   ing for a wise man, it seems that you would listen to the wisest.
7   And that would be the one who spoke the words I just read.

8   CLIMBER: *(Pause)* Huh. You mean the answer was right under
9   my nose?

10   GURU: Still is, Genius. You ought to start taking what you read a
11   bit more seriously.

12   CLIMBER: You know, for a wise man, you sure are awfully rude
13   and impatient!

14   GURU: That's why I moved up here, Ace. That, and the fact that
15   the property taxes are incredibly low ...

16   CLIMBER: Yeah, well ... thanks for the wisdom. I will pay a bit
17   more attention when I read.

18   GURU: Good. Maybe you're not so dull after all.

19   CLIMBER: Gee, thanks. This was really worth the trip!

20   GURU: Of course it was.

21   CLIMBER: *(Turns and begins the climb down.)* And thanks for the
22   guacamole recipe!

23   GURU: Courtesy of Romans 8:28. "In all things, God works for the
24   good of those who love him ..."

25   CLIMBER: The guacamole is that good?

26   GURU: Yes, it is.

27   CLIMBER: Well, OK! Thanks again! *(CLIMBER exits.)*

28   GURU: My pleasure. *(After the man is out of earshot, maybe two sec-*
29   *onds ...)* I've *got* to get an unlisted mountaintop ...

30

31

32

33

34

35

Going to Committee

A sketch on working out differences.

Theme: Conflict, disagreement

**Scripture
References:** Matthew 18:18, 1 Corinthians 1:10-11

Synopsis: A seemingly simple matter to be decided by a church committee turns into a huge ordeal.

Cast: Chairperson
Member 1
Member 2
Member 3

Props: Memo pad, four pens, offering plate.

Setting: A church committee meeting. Place a table and four chairs at Center Stage.

1   *(CHAIRPERSON and three MEMBERS sit at the table, ready for*
2   *the meeting to begin.)*
3   **CHAIRPERSON: OK, if we could go ahead and get started, we've**
4   **got a long agenda tonight, and I'd really like to get through it,**
5   **all right? OK, the first item is an easy one. The nursery needs**
6   **to be painted. Any suggestions?**
7   **MEMBER 1:** *(Raising hand)* **How 'bout we paint it?**
8   **CHAIRPERSON:** *(Looking at MEMBER 1 and slowly smiling with a*
9   *pause.)* **Yes, we should. What I meant was, we need to come up**
10   **with a color, and I wanted to know if there were any**
11   **suggestions.**
12   **MEMBER 1: Oh. What color is it now?**
13   **MEMBER 2: It's white. Well, sort of. It was white the last time we**
14   **painted it.**
15   **CHAIRPERSON: Exactly how long ago was that?**
16   **MEMBER 3: I remember! It was right before Jason was born.**
17   **MEMBER 2: How's Jason doing anyway?**
18   **MEMBER 3: Pretty good. He and his wife just celebrated their**
19   **third anniversary.**
20   **CHAIRPERSON: OK, so it's been awhile since we last painted.**
21   *(Pause)* **I say we paint it white again. Any objections?**
22   **MEMBER 2: Well, I don't know. Can't we do something different?**
23   **I mean, white is so … boring.**
24   **MEMBER 1: I agree with Larry. Nurseries** *should* **be white. It's**
25   **pure and innocent. Just like the babies that are in it!**
26   **MEMBER 3: Yeah, right. Have you seen the nursery walls? They're**
27   **anything but pure. And the white doesn't help any. We need a**
28   **change.**
29   **MEMBER 2: Yeah. How about red? That would cheer things up**
30   **a bit.**
31   **CHAIRPERSON: Red?** *(Pause)* **RED?! Are you nuts? The nursery**
32   **is supposed to be where a mother can go to take care of her**
33   **baby and relax.**
34   **MEMBER 2: Yeah? So?**
35   **CHAIRPERSON: There is nothing relaxing about red. Might as**

1   well put a stereo system on full blast back there while you're
2   at it!
3   MEMBER 1: Hey, a stereo with some nice, soft lullabies would
4   be neat ...
5   MEMBER 3: Or one of those tapes with the heartbeat in the back-
6   ground. That'd be nice ...
7   MEMBER 2: I think a music system would be cool ...
8   CHAIRPERSON: I hate to be the one to bring this up, but *(More*
9   *loudly)* WE'RE NOT TALKING ABOUT A REMODELING
10   HERE! *(Pause)* We just need to decide on a paint color for
11   the nursery.
12   MEMBER 3: I know! How about mint green?
13   MEMBER 2: Mint green? *(Pause)* You really want a church full of
14   kids that all have pistachio ice cream on their minds?
15   CHAIRPERSON: Nursing babies aren't going to be thinking about
16   pistachio ice cream!
17   MEMBER 2: They will if you paint the nursery mint green!
18   MEMBER 1: Look. If you don't want to go with white, then how
19   about a chick yellow, or something soft like that?
20   MEMBER 3: *(Softly, and rather indignantly)* Mint green is soft.
21   MEMBER 2: I read somewhere that the color yellow provokes
22   people. *(At this, they all stare silently at him for a few seconds.)*
23   MEMBER 2: What?!
24   MEMBER 1: Provokes people? Provokes people to do what?
25   MEMBER 3: Yeah, what? To spit up?
26   MEMBER 2: I don't know what! I just read it somewhere ...
27   CHAIRPERSON: Look. Let's just go with a soft blue. Who could
28   argue with a robin's egg blue?
29   MEMBER 1: Uh, well ...
30   CHAIRPERSON: Yes?
31   MEMBER 1: Isn't that kind of sexist? I mean, if we just had baby
32   boys, all right, but ...
33   CHAIRPERSON: OK, how about painting half the room blue and
34   half the room pink?
35   MEMBER 2: OK, OK ... I'm getting nauseated just picturing what

1   *that* might look like ...
2   MEMBER 3: How about peach? Peach is soft, and gender-neutral,
3   and not white ...
4   CHAIRPERSON: And very trendy.
5   MEMBER 1: Not really. Not anymore. It's out now.
6   CHAIRPERSON: Oh, great. We haven't even decided on a color
7   and already we're out of date.
8   MEMBER 3: Well, then, what do you suggest?
9   CHAIRPERSON: *(Pause)* How about wallpaper?
10 MEMBER 2: Do you really think that if we can't decide on a
11   simple color, that we're going to be able to come to consensus
12   on a wallpaper pattern?
13 MEMBER 1: We could do a border ...
14 MEMBER 3: With what as the base color?
15 CHAIRPERSON: Or a stencil ...
16 MEMBER 2: Of what? Again, who's going to decide on the stencil
17   pattern?
18 MEMBER 3: And what color goes underneath?
19   *(At this point, CHAIRPERSON collapses his head into his arms*
20   *on the table as MEMBER 1, MEMBER 2, and MEMBER 3 begin*
21   *babbling about colors and wallpapers and stencils, etc., for about*
22   *15 seconds, at which point CHAIRPERSON raises his head with*
23   *a loud voice.)*
24 CHAIRPERSON: ALL RIGHT! *(Others quiet down.)* All right. I
25   think I have a plan. It's not a good one. It's not a creative one.
26   It's not even a real plan. But it will settle this once and for all.
27 MEMBER 2: Yes?
28 CHAIRPERSON: I'm going to pass out little slips of paper. *(Passes*
29   *out torn-off pieces of his memo pad.)* I want each of you to write
30   down the color you would like to see the new nursery painted
31   and put it in this offering plate. Charla will draw one out, and
32   that will be the color of the nursery, OK? *(MEMBER 3,*
33   *MEMBER 1, and MEMBER 2 all look at each other, shrug their*
34   *shoulders and agree. After writing something on their scraps of*
35   *paper, they toss them into the plate.)* All right. I'll shake 'em up

1   a bit here. Charla? Will you do the honors?
2   MEMBER 1: My pleasure! *(MEMBER 1 draws one out and hands it*
3   *to CHAIRPERSON. He opens it up.)*
4   CHAIRPERSON: Oh, for the love of Pete! Who turned in a blank
5   piece of paper?
6   MEMBER 3: Well?!
7   MEMBER 2: What did you do that for?
8   MEMBER 3: I couldn't decide! I think the nursery color is pretty
9   important, and I didn't want to do something we'll all regret
10   later!
11   MEMBER 1: So now what are we going to do?
12   CHAIRPERSON: Wait a minute! I know!
13   MEMBER 2: What?
14   CHAIRPERSON: What color is the paper?
15   MEMBER 1: It's white.
16   CHAIRPERSON: There you go! *(Pause)* If we agreed to go with the
17   color on the paper that we drew, and no color was written,
18   then we should go with the color of the paper itself. And the
19   paper is white!
20   MEMBER 2: Works for me!
21   MEMBER 3: I suppose.
22   MEMBER 1: White it is!
23   CHAIRPERSON: All right! Finally! *(Looking at his agenda)* Now,
24   let's see. Next on the agenda is determining — *(Pause, as he*
25   *realizes how difficult this will be)* Ohhhhhh! Determining which
26   of the three pastoral candidates will be our new pastor!
27   MEMBER 1 and MEMBER 3: Oh, no!
28   MEMBER 2: Grab a piece of paper! Let's throw 'em into the plate!
29   CHAIRPERSON: Really? *(CHAIRPERSON, MEMBER 1, &*
30   *MEMBER 3 all look at each other as MEMBER 2 rips up pieces*
31   *of paper.)*
32   MEMBER 2: Sure! Worked the last time! *(CHAIRPERSON,*
33   *MEMBER 1, & MEMBER 3 all look at each other again, then*
34   *shrug and grab pieces of paper.)*
35   MEMBER 1: Works for me!

1 **MEMBER 3: Sounds like a plan!**
2 **CHAIRPERSON:** *(Pause as he writes)* **Wow! It's amazing what you**
3   **can accomplish as a team once you develop a system!**
4
5
6
7
8
9
10
11
12
13
14
15
16
17
18
19
20
21
22
23
24
25
26
27
28
29
30
31
32
33
34
35

The History of Hatred Through Time

A sketch on overcoming hatred with kindness.

Theme: Hatred, vengeance

Scripture
References: Leviticus 19:17, 1 Kings 21:20,
Proverbs 10:12, Matthew 5:38-45, Luke 6:27,
Acts 5:17-18, 1 John 2:9, 3:15

Synopsis: A number of close encounters of the hateful
kind reveal that throughout history, hatred has
never solved problems, only created them.

Cast: Narrator

(The same actor should play all these parts.)
Abel, Julius
Redcoat, Purple Guy

(The other actor should play these parts.)
Cain, Brutus
Yankee, Green Guy

Props: A large, soft club — preferably an inflatable or
Nerf bat, and a microphone (optional).

Setting: The set of a documentary television show.
Place a comfortable chair at Stage Right or
Stage Left.

1   *(A NARRATOR, similar to those found on historical or documen-*
2   *tary television shows, is at Center Stage, with a microphone [or*
3   *not]. He/she may sit in a comfortable chair off Stage Right or Left*
4   *while the historical scenes that are related take place at Center*
5   *Stage. The narrator should have a rather dry approach, perhaps*
6   *with a very stuffy accent.)*
7   **NARRATOR: Good evening, and welcome once again to** *Perspec-*
8   *tives,* **the show that looks at life through the eyes of history!**
9   **I'm your host, Wellington Rothrock, and today we'll be**
10   **exploring the history of hatred through the ages. So come with**
11   **me now as we uncover hatred at its very roots, as we peel back**
12   **the veil of ignorance and discover how to deal with this**
13   **savage emotion. Let's go!** *(He motions to the audience to follow,*
14   *perhaps repeating the gesture for effect. He then withdraws to the*
15   *side as he continues to narrate. CAIN and ABEL move to Center*
16   *Stage.)* **It seems that the first recorded incident of hatred is**
17   **found in the Bible, in the book of Genesis. In our first re-**
18   **creation, the offspring of the authors of our race have had a**
19   **slight disagreement over the favor of their offerings. Cain**
20   **feels a certain jealousy over the fact that his sacrifices are not**
21   **being recognized with as much favor as are his brother Abel's.**
22   **Let's watch!**
23   **CAIN:** *(With club hidden behind his back)* **Abel, why is it that when I**
24   **bring my offering to God, he doesn't make a fuss, but when**
25   **you bring him yours, I never hear the end of it?**
26   **ABEL: Well, let's see. I bring him leg of lamb, and ... what was it**
27   **that you brought him? Oh, that's right! Zucchini bread!**
28   *(Pause)* **Figure it out, Einstein!**
29   **CAIN: Who?**
30   **ABEL: Never mind!**
31   **CAIN: Well, it's not fair!**
32   **ABEL: Can't help you!**
33   **CAIN: Ooooh! I hate you!**
34   **ABEL: I can live with that.**
35   **CAIN: Guess again!** *(He raises club and hits ABEL over the head with*

1   *it. ABEL falls, then they freeze as NARRATOR comes from the*

2   *side to Center Stage.)*

3 NARRATOR: So from the very beginning of time, hatred has

4   resulted in tragedy! And while it seems to have had its roots in

5   jealousy, hatred knows no historical limits to its motivation.

6   Let's skip ahead now to ancient Rome, where we find Julius

7   Caesar and his supposed "friend," Brutus, engaged in a witty

8   banter ... *(He steps to the side.)*

9 JULIUS: So, Brutus, to what do I owe the honor of this visit?

10 BRUTUS: *(With club hidden behind his back)* Oh, no reason, really.

11   Can't a guy just spend the Ides of March with his best friend

12   if he wants to?

13 JULIUS: The Ides of March, did you say? Hmmm, that rings a bell.

14   No matter. I just mean that I noticed that since I have all this

15   power, there seems to be some tension between us.

16 BRUTUS: Perhaps you're right. I have been feeling a bit edgy.

17 JULIUS: Too many late night parties, Brutus?

18 BRUTUS: More like too much power on your part.

19 JULIUS: *Et tu,* Brutus? I thought you were above that!

20 BRUTUS: Not exactly, Julius. I hate you!

21 JULIUS: Oh? Well, join the club!

22 BRUTUS: I think I will! *(Clubs him.)*

23 JULIUS: *(Right after BRUTUS clubs him)* Funny — I always thought

24   I would be stabbed ... *(Falls to the ground.)*

25 BRUTUS: Sorry. Didn't have a fake knife ... *(They freeze.)*

26 NARRATOR: *(Stepping to Center Stage)* Fascinating! So, not only

27   can jealousy lead us to hatred, but the quest for power can as

28   well! Next we visit the atmosphere of war and the struggle for

29   independence in America, where hatred once again rears its

30   ugly head! *(Retreats to side.)*

31 REDCOAT: *(Pointing his pantomimed musket)* Stop, you Yankee

32   rebel, or I'll shoot!

33 YANKEE: *(Running away with his club in hand, he stops.)* All right, all

34   right! You got me!

35 REDCOAT: What were you doing down on that boat in the harbor?

1   YANKEE: I was dumping tea overboard! We're not paying your
2   stupid King's taxes!
3   REDCOAT: You fool! Do you have any idea what you've done?
4   YANKEE: Of course! The fish in that harbor will be so hyped up on
5   caffeine, we'll never catch them!
6   REDCOAT: No! *(Pause)* Well, yes! But not just that! This means war!
7   YANKEE: I don't care! I hate your country and its oppressive ways!
8   REDCOAT: It's not that oppressive, you Yankee baby!
9   YANKEE: Oh, yeah? Maybe we don't want to belong to your
10   church! Maybe we don't like crumpets! Maybe we'd rather
11   drive our carriages on the right side of the road!
12   REDCOAT: Stop talking, or I'll shoot!
13   YANKEE: Go ahead! I've had it!
14   REDCOAT: OK, I will. *(Raises his "musket" and fires, but as he does,*
15   *YANKEE hits the deck and he misses.)*
16   YANKEE: Ha, ha! You missed! And you know the terrible thing
17   about muskets?
18   REDCOAT: What?
19   YANKEE: They take forever to reload! *(He clubs him. REDCOAT*
20   *falls to the ground.)*
21   NARRATOR: *(Moving back to Center Stage)* Utterly charming!
22   Here we see that oppression can also drive someone to the
23   very brink of hatred! It seems that hatred always results in
24   violence, doesn't it? Perhaps this is why Jesus Christ, of New
25   Testament fame, was such a strong advocate of loving one's
26   enemies! If everyone lived by this principle, you would never
27   see things like this next scene happen … *(Retreats to the side.)*
28   PURPLE: *(Club in his hand, pounding his othe.)* Whatcha doing on
29   my turf, Green Boy?
30   GREEN: Who said this is your turf, Purple Dude?
31   PURPLE: Don't play ignorant with me, Greenie! You know this is
32   purple's playground, and if you don't get out of here right
33   now, I'm going to have to teach you a lesson!
34   GREEN: Oh, yeah? Well go ahead and start, Grape-head! They tell
35   me I'm a slow learner!

1   **PURPLE: I believe that! All you Green guys are stupid!**

2   **GREEN: Oh, really? I'd rather be stupid than Purple!**

3   **PURPLE: Oh, I hate you!**

4   **GREEN: I hate you too! Bring it on!**

5   **PURPLE: Say goodnight, Greenie!** *(He comes at him with the club*

6   *drawn back. As he swings the club at GREEN, GREEN ducks and*

7   *the swing misses. GREEN grabs the club, raises it and clubs PUR-*

8   *PLE. PURPLE falls to the ground.)* **Oh, man!**

9   **NARRATOR:** *(Moving back to Center Stage)***So there you have it!**

10   **Even simple differences can spark hatred! And history shows**

11   **it only leads to violence and suffering!**

12   **PURPLE:** *(Rising to his feet)* **Yeah. Most of it mine! How come I**

13   **always get clobbered?**

14   **GREEN: Sorry. It's nothing personal. It was in the script ...**

15   **NARRATOR:** *(Ignoring them)* **It seems that the only answer to**

16   **hatred would be to avoid it at all costs. Certainly, as we have**

17   **seen here today, it is always destructive.**

18   **PURPLE: Whose idea was it, then?**

19   **GREEN: I think it was that guy.** *(Points to NARRATOR.)*

20   **NARRATOR:** *(Nervously)* **Uh, yes. Well, join us next time on**

21   *Perspectives* **when we look at the history of forgiveness!**

22   **PURPLE: Who is that guy, anyway? I hate him!**

23   **GREEN: Me too!**

24   **PURPLE: Let's get him!**

25   **NARRATOR: I'm your host, Wellington Rothrock, and I did NOT**

26   **write the script!** *(Exits hurriedly, with others chasing him.)*

27

28

29

30

31

32

33

34

35

How Much Farther?

A sketch on running the good race.

Theme: Perseverance, encouragement

Scripture References: Matthew 24:13, Hebrews 12:1

Synopsis: A runner who threatens to quit the race is given encouragement to continue.

Cast: Runner 1
Runner 2

Props: None.

Setting: A race course.

1   *(Two RUNNERS, more if they are available, run across the stage,*
2   *but RUNNER 2 stops halfway across, panting heavily and putting*
3   *his hands on his knees. RUNNER 1, after running across the*
4   *stage, comes back to encourage RUNNER 2.)*
5   **RUNNER 1: Hey, man, what are you doing? We're only halfway done!**
6   **RUNNER 2:** *(Panting heavily)* **Go on, man! Finish the race.**
7   *(Panting)* **I can't do it.**
8   **RUNNER 1: Don't say that, guy! You can do it!**
9   **RUNNER 2: No way!** *(Panting)* **I'll never make it!**
10   **RUNNER 1: Come on, now! We've both trained for this for a long**
11   **time. I know how important it is to you.**
12   **RUNNER 2:** *(Panting)* **It was important. *Was*. But it's just too hard.**
13   **RUNNER 1: Are you forgetting that feeling of finishing the race**
14   **that we've always dreamed of?**
15   **RUNNER 2:** *(Panting)* **Right now? Yes. I'm forgetting.**
16   **RUNNER 1: You can't do that! I won't let you!**
17   **RUNNER 2:** *(Glaring at him)* **Why *not*?**
18   **RUNNER 1: Look. I know that at one time, you wanted this as**
19   **much as I did.**
20   **RUNNER 2: That was a long time ago. Like, back at the starting line.**
21   **RUNNER 1: That wasn't *that* long ago, man.**
22   **RUNNER 2: I suppose not. But I just can't do it.**
23   **RUNNER 1: Sure you can! You know how bad you're going to feel**
24   **if you don't finish?**
25   **RUNNER 2: Can't imagine it would be worse than right now!**
26   **RUNNER 1: Well, it will be! There's nothing worse than knowing**
27   **that you could've done something if you would've tried just a**
28   **little harder.**
29   **RUNNER 2: No, I suppose you're right.**
30   **RUNNER 1: Of course I'm right! We've talked about this for a**
31   **long time.**
32   **RUNNER 2: Yeah, we *have* been meaning to do this for a long time.**
33   **RUNNER 1: Forever. And we never talked about not finishing the**
34   **race, did we?**
35   **RUNNER 2: No, I guess we never did.**

1   RUNNER 1: Look. Just imagine crossing the finish line ...
2   RUNNER 2: Yeah?
3   RUNNER 1: Imagine how good it's going to feel to stop at the end
4   of the race and know that you gave it your best shot!
5   RUNNER 2: That *would* feel good ...
6   RUNNER 1: And hearing the guy there at the finish line say,
7   "Good race!"
8   RUNNER 2: That'd be cool.
9   RUNNER 1: Cool? There will be nothing like it!
10   RUNNER 2: I suppose not.
11   RUNNER 1: And best of all, after you try your hardest and cross
12   that line, imagine how good it's going to feel to sit down and
13   rest, knowing it's over.
14   RUNNER 2: I can feel it now!
15   RUNNER 1: So you'll finish?
16   RUNNER 2: *(Pause)* You bet!
17   RUNNER 1: That's the spirit!
18   RUNNER 2: Well, what are we waiting for? Let's finish the race!
19   RUNNER 1: All right!
20   RUNNER 2: How far do you suppose we have left?
21   RUNNER 1: Oh, about half. Just past that tree up there.
22   RUNNER 2: That's all?
23   RUNNER 1: Well, it is just the one hundred-meter dash. *(He takes off.)*
24   RUNNER 2: *(Pause)* Man, I gotta get into shape! *(He starts to run*
25   *Off-stage.)*
26   RUNNER 1: *(From Off-stage)* Yes, you do!
27
28
29
30
31
32
33
34
35

How Then Shall We Live?

A sketch on the responsibilities of freedom.

Theme: Freedom

Scripture References: Matthew 24:13, Hebrews 12:1

Synopsis: Three prisoners are pardoned. Two of them jump at the chance for freedom. But a third stubbornly stays put, insisting it's only a matter of time before they end up right back in the cell.

Cast: Prisoner 1
Prisoner 2
Prisoner 3
Warden

Props: A cup.

Setting: A jail cell. Place three folding chairs at Center Stage.

1   *(PRISONERS 1 & 2 sit at Center Stage. PRISONER 3 stands, try-*
2   *ing to listen through the wall with a cup.)*
3   **PRISONER 1:** *(Singing)* **Nobody knows the trouble I've seen ...**
4   **PRISONER 2: Would ya shut up with that song already? In the**
5   **first place, that's the thousandth time you've sung that stupid**
6   **song. And in the second place, we all know the trouble you've**
7   **seen — we've seen it too!**
8   **PRISONER 1: Well excuse me for being depressed about being in**
9   **prison! You want I should dance?**
10 **PRISONER 3:** *(Trying to listen through the wall with a cup)* **Shhhh!**
11   *(Pause)* **I can't believe it!**
12 **PRISONER 2: What?**
13 **PRISONER 3: We're going to be free!**
14 **PRISONER 1: What? You're kidding!**
15 **PRISONER 3: We're to be released today! We're free!**
16 **PRISONER 1: But how?**
17 **PRISONER 3: I don't know.** *(Pause, while listening)* **Someone ... has**
18   **pardoned us, it seems.**
19 **PRISONER 1: Wow! Free again!**
20 **PRISONER 2:** *(Muttering)* **Big deal ...**
21 **PRISONER 3:** *(Sitting)* **What's wrong, Sid? Didn't you hear me?**
22   **I said we're free ...**
23 **PRISONER 2: Yeah, I heard you.**
24 **PRISONER 1:** *(Pause)* **So how's come you're not excited about**
25   **gettin' out? We been in here a long time, you and me.**
26 **PRISONER 2: Yeah, we have. And I'll be in here for a lot longer.**
27 **PRISONER 3: No! We are** *all* **to be freed. Everyone in this cell**
28   **block. I heard it ...**
29 **PRISONER 2: I don't care what you heard.** *(Pause)* *I'm* **not going.**
30 **PRISONER 1: How's come, Sid?**
31 **PRISONER 2: Look. I been in here longer than you guys, right?**
32 **PRISONERS 1 & 3:** *(Together)* **Yeah, so?**
33 **PRISONER 2: So, you may get out. Big deal. You'll be right back**
34   **in, probably within the week.**
35 **PRISONER 3: Not me! I can do right this time. I can stay clean.**

1   PRISONER 2: Yeah, whatever. No one stays clean. It ain't natural.

2   PRISONER 1: Well, maybe we can stay clean enough to stay free.

3   PRISONER 2: Give me a break. Sooner or later, you'll be back. So

4   I'm not wastin' the time. I'm staying.

5   PRISONER 3: But that's crazy! Who in the world would choose this

6   over freedom?

7   PRISONER 2: Me, that's who. *(Nodding at one, then the other)* **And**

8   **you. And you too, eventually.**

9   PRISONER 1: You really think we can't be free, Sid? I mean, I

10   don't like being a prisoner — you know that. And I don't

11   think you do, either ....

12   PRISONER 2: Maybe not. But it's a lot easier than getting out.

13   PRISONER 3: What could be easier than accepting a pardon?

14   PRISONER 2: You know anybody who's been pardoned?

15   PRISONER 3: Sure I do. Lots of people.

16   PRISONER 2: And anybody that stayed clean? I mean really?

17   PRISONER 1: *(Pause)* But we're being given a pardon. We'd be

18   foolish not to take it.

19   PRISONER 2: Lots of people don't. *(WARDEN comes up and opens*

20   *the imaginary gates. PRISONER 3 goes out immediately.)*

21   PRISONER 3: Come on, you guys. We're free!

22   PRISONER 1: *(Looking back at PRISONER 2 while stepping through*

23   *door)* Come on, Sid. It's freedom!

24   PRISONER 2: I don't think so. Not this time. I'll see you suckers in

25   a couple of weeks.

26   PRISONER 3: Not me, Sid. I'm going to make the most of this

27   chance, even if I don't deserve it. *(Exits.)*

28   PRISONER 1: I hate being a prisoner, Sid. I gotta try! You sure you

29   won't come?

30   PRISONER 2: *(Shaking his head)* You'll see. Freedom has too many

31   responsibilities. You'll be back. *(PRISONER 1 looks longingly*

32   *back at PRISONER 2 before exiting.)*

33   WARDEN: Suit yourself. *(Slams imaginary door shut.)*

34   PRISONER 2: *(After long pause, sitting in cell, begins singing)*

35   Nobody knows the trouble I've seen ...

I Do ... Don't I?

A sketch looking at doubt.

Theme: Doubt

**Scripture
References:** Mark 11:22-23, John 20:27

Synopsis: A bride who is anxious about her impending lifetime commitment receives calm assurance from her maid of honor.

Cast: Maid of Honor
Bride

Props: None.

Setting: A changing room prior to a wedding. A veil and wedding dress may be hanging up in the background (optional).

1   *(The BRIDE stands at Center Stage, looking rather anxious. In*
2   *walks the MAID OF HONOR.)*
3   **MAID OF HONOR: Oh, Julie! This is it! The big day!**
4   **BRIDE: Don't remind me.**
5   **MAID OF HONOR: What? And by the way, shouldn't you be**
6   **getting ready by now?**
7   **BRIDE: You'd think so. But obviously, I'm not ready.**
8   **MAID OF HONOR: I hope you're just talking about getting**
9   **dressed ...**
10   **BRIDE: Yeah, me too.**
11   **MAID OF HONOR: Oh, come on, Julie. You're not getting cold**
12   **feet, are you?**
13   **BRIDE: If my feet were any colder, they'd be out there floating in**
14   **the punch bowl.**
15   **MAID OF HONOR: I don't understand. You don't want to get**
16   **married?**
17   **BRIDE: Oh, I don't know. I mean, of course I do! But it's such a**
18   **commitment. This is for *life.***
19   **MAID OF HONOR: Well, we would hope so. Why are you ques-**
20   **tioning things now?**
21   **BRIDE: Well, I don't know! I mean, how do you know if the one**
22   **you're about to give the rest of your life to is really who he says**
23   **he is?**
24   **MAID OF HONOR: Do what I do. Ask for ID.**
25   **BRIDE: Which is exactly why you're not my MATRON of honor.**
26   **I'm serious.**
27   **MAID OF HONOR: Oh, I know. But why are you doubting him**
28   **now? He's a great guy!**
29   **BRIDE: Yes, that's just it. He seems too good to be true. But how do**
30   **I know? He seems to have all the things I want in a husband,**
31   **but I can't know his heart. I can't see his thoughts. I have to**
32   **trust him.**
33   **MAID OF HONOR: And you don't?**
34   **BRIDE: Well ... I do, but ... it's just impossible to know if I'm**
35   **making a mistake, isn't it? I mean, if I could see the future —**

1   know exactly what would happen …
2   MAID OF HONOR: But you know that's impossible.
3   BRIDE: Which is exactly why I need wool socks right now. *(Pause)*
4   I *can't* know for sure.
5   MAID OF HONOR: Look. You've known him for years, right?
6   BRIDE: Right.
7   MAID OF HONOR: Has he ever let you down?
8   BRIDE: Well, no. Not with anything big …
9   MAID OF HONOR: And hasn't your life been full of joy and hope
10   since then?
11   BRIDE: Yes, but that doesn't count. Joy is his mother's name and
12   Hope is his sister!
13   MAID OF HONOR: OK, bad example. But you are happy when
14   you're with him, right?
15   BRIDE: Yes, of course. He makes me very happy.
16   MAID OF HONOR: Then?
17   BRIDE: I just need proof that he's really the man he claims to be.
18   Something … tangible.
19   MAID OF HONOR: It doesn't work that way. You're just going to
20   have to believe in him. Or learn to live alone. Without Hope
21   and Joy.
22   BRIDE: Actually, that wouldn't always be a bad thing. But
23   seriously. That takes a whole lot of faith.
24   MAID OF HONOR: That's what faith is. If you could see it, it
25   would be … advertising. And you know how much truth there
26   is in that!
27   BRIDE: I suppose you're right. Do you think I'm doing the
28   right thing?
29   MAID OF HONOR: How would I know? The only guy I trust is my
30   dad. But I think so.
31   BRIDE: Oh … I know you're right. It's just hard to have that
32   much faith.
33   MAID OF HONOR: Well, if it makes you feel better, if you decide
34   not to marry him, *I will.*
35   BRIDE: Now *that*, I doubt!

I Humbly Accept This Award...

A sketch on true humility.

Theme: Humility

Scripture References: Colossians 2:18, Luke 14:11

Synopsis: At the "Most Humble" award ceremony, several hecklers question the authenticity of the recipient. If he really *was* humble, wouldn't he refuse the award?

Cast: MC
Mr. Wilson (or a member of your congregation)
Heckler 1
Heckler 2
Heckler 3

Props: Several pages of notes.

Setting: A church awards banquet.

1   *(A master of ceremonies [MC] is directing the proceedings at a*
2   *church awards banquet. He calls up a person to receive the "Most*
3   *Humble" award. [Note: A variation of the setting is that you use*
4   *your own church service as the setting and set up the award to be*
5   *given to a member of your congregation as a part of the service*
6   *itself. The congregation then acts as the award ceremony crowd.]*
7   *Three HECKLERS are planted in the congregation to question the*
8   *speaker's humility.)*
9   **MC:** *(Clapping)* **Thank you, Mr. Johnson, for your eloquent accep-**
10   **tance of the "Most Quiet Spirit" award. I'm sure that all**
11   **among us who could actually hear it were quite moved.**
12   *(Pause)* **Our church regularly awards one of our members the**
13   **next award for demonstrating outstanding humility in their**
14   **service to the church. For the fourth year in a row, the award**
15   **goes to ...** *(Insert member's name, or)* **Mr. Keith Wilson!** *(Claps*
16   *as MR. WILSON stands and approaches the podium.)*
17   **MR. WILSON: Thank you! Thank you! It is with great humility**
18   **that I accept this award, given by my peers as an esteemed**
19   **token of your recognition of my humble spirit. I shall place**
20   **the trophy next to the other three on my mantle and be**
21   **humbled whenever I walk by them.** *(Chuckles.)* **But seriously,**
22   **I am reminded once again of the honor that this brings to our**
23   **church and to myself as a member here. Humility, true**
24   **humility, must be sought after with the intensity of a great**
25   **athlete, say, a Michael Jordan. And even though Michael**
26   **Jordan may be the greatest athlete on his or any other team,**
27   **he still needs the rest of his team to win. That is why it is for**
28   **our entire team that I proudly accept this award. In a humble**
29   **kind of a way, that is. For it is only through humility that we**
30   **can truly know ...** *(He is interrupted by HECKLER 1 midway*
31   *through the last sentence.)*
32   **HECKLER 1: Excuse me, Mr. Wilson?**
33   **MR. WILSON: Uh, I've just got a few more humble things to say,**
34   **so could this wait?**
35   **HECKLER 1: Well, sure, but I was just curious about something ...**

1   MR. WILSON: Good. As I was saying, to be truly humble, you have
2   to take a great deal of pride *(HECKLER 1 interrupts here.)* in
3   how humble you truly are —
4   HECKLER 1: Excuse me, Mr. Wilson?
5   MR. WILSON: Now what?
6   HECKLER 1: Well, I just have a question. About being humble,
7   I mean.
8   MR. WILSON: This is an acceptance speech, if you don't mind! Not
9   a press conference!
10   HECKLER 1: Well, that's just it. Can you really make a speech
11   about being humble if you truly are?
12   MR. WILSON: Well, not if I get interrupted too often —
13   HECKLER 1: No, not you, specifically. Can anyone really accept an
14   award for humility?
15   MR. WILSON: What do you mean?
16   HECKLER 1: Well, it seems to me that if you truly were humble,
17   you would refuse to accept an award on humility, much less
18   expect it ...
19   MR. WILSON: What makes you think I expected it?
20   HECKLER: Your three pages of notes, for one thing.
21   MR. WILSON: *(Pause)* Well, I'm just very prepared ...
22   HECKLER 1: I just think to be truly humble is to put everyone else
23   before yourself and make yourself last. I don't think you would
24   accept an award for humility, if you really were humble.
25   MR. WILSON: Uh, I uh ... well, it goes so well with the other
26   three ...
27   HECKLER 2: Hey, I think she's right. I want to change my vote, too.
28   MR. WILSON: Hey, wait a minute! You can't change your vote ...
29   HECKLER 3: Me too! He's not so humble!
30   MR. WILSON: Now, just a second. *(Pause)* Maybe you're right.
31   HECKLER 1: How do you mean?
32   MR. WILSON: I mean, I think I see your point.
33   HECKLER 3: You do?
34   MR. WILSON: I do. And I don't deserve this award.
35   HECKLER 1: Really?

1   MR. WILSON: That's right. If I did, I wouldn't accept it.

2   HECKLER 1: That's what I mean!

3   MR. WILSON: I would give this award to everyone in the church

4   before I accepted it myself.

5   HECKLER 3: That's better!

6   MR. WILSON: And even then, I wouldn't take it.

7   HECKLER 1: It would be hypocritical.

8   MR. WILSON: So it is with great humility that I decline your

9   gracious award.

10 HECKLER 2: That's more like it!

11 MR. WILSON: *(Starts to walk Off-stage, then stops and returns.)* **Now**

12   that I've proven my humility, can I ...

13 ALL HECKLERS: *(Together)* No! *(MR. WILSON walks Off-stage*

14   *quickly.)*

15

16

17

18

19

20

21

22

23

24

25

26

27

28

29

30

31

32

33

34

35

In Honor of Parents?

*A sketch about parents and their
relationships with their kids.*

Theme: Parental relationships

**Scripture
Reference:** Ephesians 6:1-4

Synopsis: A video walk down memory lane is not quite
the family bonding experience that Dad had
hoped for.

Cast: Dad
Mom
Kid 1
Kid 2

Props: TV remote.

Setting: The family room. Place four chairs at Center
Stage.

1 (*DAD enters, followed by MOM, and then reluctantly by*
2 *KID 1 & KID 2. All of them are moving toward seating arrange-*
3 *ments that would simulate being in front of a TV; they face the*
4 *audience. DAD begins talking before they are even seated.*)
5 **DAD: All right, kids, are you ready? This is gonna be a blast!**
6 **KID 1: Dad, are you sure we couldn't get you something *else* for**
7 **Father's Day? *Please!***
8 **DAD: Like what? I don't need anything else. Besides, this is what I**
9 **want — to spend time with my family, remembering all the**
10 **great times we've had!**
11 **KID 2. Oh, brother …**
12 **MOM: Are you sure, dear? I mean, if the kids would rather get you**
13 **a tie or something …**
14 **DAD: What's wrong with you guys? Can't a father just reminisce**
15 **with his family about the great times they've had without**
16 **being the bad guy? Besides, you said I could have whatever I**
17 **wanted, and this is what I want.**
18 **MOM: OK, dear, but don't say I didn't warn you …**
19 **DAD: About what? What could be the harm in this? It'll bring us**
20 **closer together. Now, let's watch — I've put all of our video**
21 **highlights from the last few years together.**
22 **KID 1 & KID 2: Oh, no …** (*They both throw their heads back in exas-*
23 *peration.*) **Why us?**
24 **DAD: I SAID HIGHLIGHTS!** (*Smiling sweetly, regaining compo-*
25 *sure*) **It's really not that long. Humor your old man, would**
26 **you? Hand me the remote.** (*KID 1 does.*)
27 **MOM: Oh, look! It's our vacation to Mexico three years ago!**
28 **DAD: That's right! Now wasn't that a blast?** (*Pause, as all three*
29 *stare at him.*)
30 **DAD: What?!**
31 **KID 1: Dad, that was the worst family vacation in history.**
32 **DAD: It wasn't that bad.**
33 **KID 2: Oh, no. Not that bad. "The water's fine, the water's fine,"**
34 **you said. I've never been so sick in my life.**
35 **KID 1: Not to mention that time-share thing we all had to sit**

1   through for three hours.

2   DAD: But we got to go on that free cruise, remember?

3   KID 2: I remember drinking about a gallon of water before we left.

4   *(KID 1 and KID 2 look at each other and make sick faces.)* **I don't**

5   **remember much about the cruise.**

6   MOM: Perhaps we'd better move on, dear.

7   DAD: Oh, all right. *(Fast-forwards for a few seconds while talking.)*

8   But I still think it was a fun vacation, driving all over, looking

9   for Mayan ruins ...

10   KID 1: Dad, we never found any Mayan ruins. You wouldn't let us

11   ask where any were.

12   MOM: We were lost for hours!

13   DAD: Oh, we found ruins! Remember the statue I found?

14   KID 2: Dad, that was a rock that happened to bear a resemblance

15   to a head.

16   KID 1: Richard Nixon's.

17   DAD: It was a Mayan sculpture. Oh wait. ... *(Stops fast-forwarding.)*

18   Look, Jonathan. It's your middle school graduation!

19   KID 1: Keep fast-forwarding, please!

20   MOM: Oh, isn't he cute?!

21   KID 1: Here we go.

22   DAD: Now that was a fun family memory, right?

23   KID 1: Are you kidding? I wanted to die, you embarrassed me so

24   badly!

25   DAD: What?

26   KID 1: Dad, you stood up and yelled, "There goes a future U.S.

27   president!" right when they announced my name.

28   DAD: So? It could still happen!

29   KID 1: I don't want to be president! And all my friends were

30   laughing.

31   MOM: Well, if they were laughing at you, dear ...

32   MOM, KID 1 and KID 2: *(Together)* They're not real friends!

33   DAD: All right, let's move on. *(Fast-forwarding)*

34   KID 1: Hey, there's Dad giving you driving lessons, Annika! That

35   was hilarious!

1   DAD: Let's move on.

2   KID 2: Hey, your time's coming. I'll be surprised if you make it.

3   KID 1: What do you mean by that?

4   MOM: Kids!

5   DAD: I said, let's move on!

6   KID 2: Well, see there when Dad is driving and I'm riding along,

7   learning from him?

8   KID 1: Yeah?

9   DAD: Won't this thing go any faster?

10   KID 2: Dad got a ticket for making an illegal lane change. *(All*

11   *laugh.)* "Do as I say, not as I do," he says.

12   DAD: All right, the show's over.

13   KID 1 and KID 2: Good. We're outta here!

14   MOM: Where are you going?

15   KID 1: To the mall.

16   DAD: But we're not done having our family time!

17   KID 2: I think we *are*. See you guys later!

18   DAD: Wait, I've got another tape — it's much better! *(They exit.)* It

19   was from back before you learned how to talk! *(Turning*

20   *around to sit back down, DAD is quickly engrossed in the video.)*

21   MOM: Kids today. Where do they learn how to ignore their

22   parents so well? *(Pause)* Dear? *(Pause)* DEAR!

23   DAD: *(Startled into attention)* Huh? What?

24

25

26

27

28

29

30

31

32

33

34

35

The Incredible Waste-O-Matic

A sketch emphasizing that if bad things go in,
bad fruit is the result.

Theme: Fruitfulness

Scripture
Reference: Matthew 12:33-35

Synopsis: A wacky scientist's latest invention makes brownies out of garbage — with dubious results.

Cast: Hope
Dr. Wizard

Props: A brownie (or it may be pantomimed).

Sound
Effects: Machine noises (taped or created Off-stage).

Setting: Mr. Wizard's lab. His Waste-O-Matic machine, which should resemble a garbage heap, sits at Center Stage. It may be three-dimensional, painted cardboard, or imaginary.

1   (*MR. WIZARD is at Center Stage, tinkering with his machine.*
2   *HOPE enters.*)
3   HOPE: Hey, Mr. Wizard! Whatcha doing?
4   MR. WIZARD: Hey, Hope! You're just in time to be the first to
5   sample the product of my latest invention!
6   HOPE: (*Looking at the invention curiously*) ... Which is?
7   MR. WIZARD: The incredible Waste-O-Matic food processor!
8   HOPE: Food processor?
9   MR. WIZARD: Yep! Well, it's not your traditional food processor.
10   It turns ordinary table scraps into delicious, nutritious
11   brownies.
12   HOPE: Really?
13   MR. WIZARD: Yep! It's going to make me a fortune!
14   HOPE: But how can it work? I mean, in order to get good things
15   out of something, don't you have to put good things in?
16   MR. WIZARD: Not anymore!
17   HOPE: I don't know, Mr. Wizard. The Bible says that if you store
18   up bad things in your heart, that's what will come out. It
19   seems to me that the same thing would happen here, unless
20   you put something good in too.
21   MR. WIZARD: Well, that's the beauty of my machine. You don't
22   have to put anything good in.
23   HOPE: Then how can you possibly expect to get anything good out?
24   MR. WIZARD: Science!
25   HOPE: But Mr. Wizard, that doesn't make any sense!
26   MR. WIZARD: It doesn't have to make any sense! It makes
27   brownies!
28   HOPE: I don't think so!
29   MR. WIZARD: Watch! I've already loaded it up! (*MR. WIZARD*
30   *flips a switch and the machine rumbles to life. The sounds coming*
31   *from it can be made with the use of a tape recorder or someone*
32   *backstage.*)
33   HOPE: What did you put in it?
34   MR. WIZARD: Well, all kinds of things. Orange peels, potato skins,
35   newspaper, rotten eggs, chicken bones, junk mail ... anything

1   **that has no value. That's what makes it such a great machine!**

2   **No more garbage! You put it in here and then you eat it!**

3   *(Pause)* **Sounds like it's almost done!**

4   **HOPE: Sounds like it's almost nauseating! That stuff couldn't be**

5   **very good for you!**

6   **MR. WIZARD: Good for you, *and* good tasting!** *(Ding Off-stage or*

7   *on tape as the machine noise stops. MR. WIZARD reaches behind*

8   *the machine and pulls out a brownie or pantomimes one.)* **You get**

9   **to be the first one to try it!**

10   **HOPE: No, thanks! I think I'm going back and reading that**

11   **Scripture first. I think I'd believe the Bible before I trust some**

12   **crazy invention!** *(She walks Off-stage.)*

13   **MR. WIZARD:** *(Yelling after her)* **Suit yourself! But you're passing**

14   **up a piece of history!** *(Eyes the brownie in his hand momentarily*

15   *before shrugging his shoulders.)* **Here goes nothing!** *(He takes a*

16   *bite and chews carelessly and smiles smugly, then more slowly as*

17   *the grin disappears. He should try and utter a few "Yuk!" noises.*

18   *He should make it obvious that it is not pleasant, perhaps even*

19   *chewing with his mouth open to the audience before a very forced*

20   *swallow, acting like he is trying to keep from gagging. After he is*

21   *able to swallow, he wipes his mouth.)* **Hope! What was that**

22   **Scripture again?** *(He exits stage.)*

23

24

25

26

27

28

29

30

31

32

33

34

35

Is This in My Job Description?

A sketch for Mother's Day.

Theme: Mothers

**Scripture
References:** Ephesians 6:2, Proverbs 23:22,
Matthew 7:10, 10:19

Synopsis: A panel of three interviewers tries to land a candidate from a recently vacated position without much hope for success.

Cast: Interviewer 1
Interviewer 2
Interviewer 3
Candidate

Props: Calculator.

Setting: A conference room. Set up a table at an angle, so all the characters are visible to the audience. Place three chairs on one side for the Interviewers, and one chair on the other side for the Candidate.

1   *(The INTERVIEWERS sit at the table. CANDIDATE enters.)*

2   **CANDIDATE: Hi! I'm, uh, answering your ad in the paper.**

3   **INTERVIEWER 1: Certainly, Mr. ...**

4   **CANDIDATE: Williams. Gary Williams.**

5   **INTERVIEWER 1: Have a seat, Mr. Williams.**

6   **CANDIDATE: Thanks. So, your ad wasn't very specific — what**

7   **exactly are you looking for?**

8   **INTERVIEWER 2: Well, it's a really varied position. It would be**

9   **something new every day.**

10   **INTERVIEWER 3: That's right. There are a lot of functions that**

11   **we're looking for. I guess the position is best compared to a**

12   **creative management position.**

13   **INTERVIEWER 1: Yeah, management. You'll be overseeing a**

14   **group of four individuals and coordinating basically every**

15   **aspect of their lives.**

16   **CANDIDATE: Wow. Sounds like a lot of responsibility. Tell me more.**

17   **INTERVIEWER 2: You'll be responsible for scheduling daily**

18   **activities for all of these individuals, down to the most minute**

19   **detail, like setting up doctor and dentist appointments, extra-**

20   **curricular activities, etc. ...**

21   **INTERVIEWER 1: And providing them with chauffeured trans-**

22   **portation to those appointments as well.**

23   **CANDIDATE: Excuse me?**

24   **INTERVIEWER 3: Oh, don't worry — we provide the vehicle. A**

25   **1995 Plymouth Voyager. Very nice!**

26   **INTERVIEWER 1: Anyway, you'll also be responsible for main-**

27   **taining inventory — you know, things like food, cleaning**

28   **supplies, toiletries, wardrobe — for the individuals you'll be**

29   **supervising ...**

30   **INTERVIEWER 2: As well as meal preparation, general household**

31   **maintenance, immediate supervision when necessary ....**

32   **INTERVIEWER 3: And a constant supply of chocolate chip cookies.**

33   **INTERVIEWER 1 and INTERVIEWER 2: Jonathan! Shhhh!**

34   **INTERVIEWER 3: Hey, no cookies, no deal!**

35   **CANDIDATE: Couldn't I delegate any of these responsibilities to**

1   the people under me? *(All of them look at each other and snicker,*
2   *but then regain composure.)*
3   INTERVIEWER 1: You may certainly give it your best shot …
4   INTERVIEWER 3: You'll also need to be available for crisis coun-
5   seling, and some mediation when necessary.
6   INTERVIEWER 2: And you'll need some medical knowledge —
7   are you CPR certified?
8   CANDIDATE: Well …
9   INTERVIEWER 3: Let's talk a little about the hours. You'll work
10   six a.m. to nine p.m. on the weekdays, and probably until mid-
11   night on the weekends …
12   CANDIDATE: Weekends?! How many hours are we talking here?
13   INTERVIEWER 1: *(Doing some math)* Approximately one hundred
14   fifteen a week. Whoa! Is that right?
15   INTERVIEWER 2: But of course you'll be on call the rest of
16   the time …
17   CANDIDATE: What?
18   INTERVIEWER 3: Don't worry — there is some down-time in
19   there … somewhere …
20   CANDIDATE: May I ask exactly what the job pays?
21   INTERVIEWER 1: Room and board.
22   CANDIDATE: Excuse me?
23   INTERVIEWER 3: And whatever's left of the money that you're
24   given to cover expenses.
25   CANDIDATE: Which would be …
26   INTERVIEWER 1: *(Doing the math)* Approximately 22 cents an
27   hour. *(Smacks the calculator on the table as CANDIDATE begins*
28   *to rise to exit.)* But it's tax-free!
29   INTERVIEWER 2: *(Rising, pleading)* And you're welcome to take
30   on another job in your spare time to supplement, as long as
31   you use some of it for expenses …
32   CANDIDATE: I think I've wasted enough of my time …
33   INTERVIEWER 3: Wait! Did we mention the three-week vacation
34   you get to plan … *(Fading as CANDIDATE disappears)*
35   INTERVIEWER 1: Darn! That's the sixteenth one today!

1   **INTERVIEWER 2: Face it, Tim, this isn't going to work. If we**
2   **don't apologize to Mom real soon, we're going to end up hav-**
3   **ing to do this stuff ourselves!** *(All gasp and exit quickly to find*
4   *Mom, perhaps even asking for her as they exit.)*

5
6
7
8
9
10
11
12
13
14
15
16
17
18
19
20
21
22
23
24
25
26
27
28
29
30
31
32
33
34
35

It's Your Serve

A sketch on serving God where you are.

Theme: Service

Scripture References: Romans 12:13, 1 Timothy 3:2

Synopsis: When a motorist's tire goes flat, she encounters two cars that drive on by. Then one sympathetic driver finally helps her (albeit bumblingly). The mission field is as close as your local freeway!

Cast: Driver 1
Driver 2
Driver 3
Driver 4
Passenger

Props: None.

Sound Effects: A loud thump, simulating a flat tire.

Setting: A freeway.

1   *(All characters mimic driving a car as they cross the stage.*
2   *DRIVER 1 enters from Stage Left.)*
3   **DRIVER 1:** *(Having an incredibly bad day, obviously distressed)* **Good**
4   **grief! I am so tired of this ... life! My job stinks, my marriage**
5   **stinks, I have no friends — even my *goldfish* ran away! I have**
6   **no idea what my life is all about.** *(Looking skyward)* **God? Are**
7   **you even up there?** *(There is a loud thumping sound as her tire*
8   *goes flat.)* **Oh, great! A flat tire! That's all I need! If this is**
9   **supposed to be some sort of sign, God, you've got a terrible**
10   **sense of timing!** *(Slumps over in despair, car stalled at Center*
11   *Stage.)*
12   **DRIVER 2:** *(Whistling a happy tune as he drives in from Stage Right)*
13   **Wow, what a great day!** *(Insert local Christian Radio station)* **is**
14   **playing all my favorite songs, my boss noticed what a great job**
15   **I've been doing, and God is really doing wonderful things in**
16   **my life! It is so good to know that you are doing just the thing**
17   **God wants you to be doing. And I'm right on schedule for the**
18   **worship planning meeting, too! I've got some great ideas for**
19   **the service on "serving God where you are" next Sunday.**
20   *(Noticing the stalled car)* **Oooh! That's too bad! That's why I**
21   **check my tires for nails every time I get behind the wheel! I'll**
22   **bet they were probably on their way to something important,**
23   **too. They'll be late now, I guess.** *(Glancing at watch)* **So will I**
24   **if I don't get moving!** *(He disappears from sight.)*
25   **DRIVER 3:** *(Two people in car enter from Stage Right, laughing.)*
26   **That's a pretty good one! I didn't even know they *had* Amish**
27   **electricians!**
28   **PASSENGER: Well, that's what makes it funny ...**
29   **DRIVER 3: Yeah, I guess you're right.** *(Pause)* **Hey, you coming to**
30   **church this Sunday?**
31   **PASSENGER: I dunno. Did you hear what the sermon was about?**
32   **DRIVER 3: It's on serving God where you are. You know, like**
33   **blooming where you're planted, or something.**
34   **PASSENGER: Oh. That's always tough. You know, I try to be Christ-**
35   **like every day, but it's hard to know what that is most of the time.**

1   DRIVER 3: Yeah, I ... hey, look at that lady. Looks like she needs
2   help, huh?
3   PASSENGER: Yup. Hope she gets it.
4   DRIVER 3: Do you think we should stop?
5   PASSENGER: Are you kidding me? Don't you read the papers? That's
6   how aliens abduct people — by posing as stranded motorists!
7   Besides, I have a cousin who has a friend, and her sister's thera-
8   pist had a son who stopped to help someone with a flat, and ...
9   DRIVER 3: And they were kidnapped and never heard from again,
10   right?
11   PASSENGER: *(Pause)* No. Actually, he fixed the flat, but the tire
12   iron fell on his foot, and he still walks with a limp when it rains.
13   DRIVER 3: *(Digesting this information)* Well, it probably isn't too safe
14   out there. And besides, it's so nice and air-conditioned in here.
15   PASSENGER: And so hot out there. I'll encourage her, though. *(He*
16   *waves at her enthusiastically.)*
17   DRIVER 3: Yeah, that probably makes her feel a *lot* better ... *(They*
18   *disappear from sight.)*
19   DRIVER 1: You know, I'm really starting to despise people ... *(She*
20   *buries her head in her hands.)*
21   DRIVER 4: *(Driver 4 enters from Stage Right, mumbling to herself.)*
22   Man! I'm gonna be late for the planning meeting again! Oh,
23   well, it's not like they expect me on time. I guess I really need to
24   get my life in order. I mean, this week's sermon is on serving
25   God where you are. Ha! What do I know about serving God?
26   Come to think of it, how do I know where I am most of the
27   time? Well, not anymore! I'm resolving myself to look for
28   ways that I can serve God, instead of sitting alongside the
29   road like that person over there. Hey, wait a minute! That
30   person looks like they're in trouble. *(Pulls off to the side of the*
31   *road and gets out.)* Hi! You need help?
32   DRIVER 1: Oh, thank goodness! I was beginning to think I'd be out
33   here all day!
34   DRIVER 4: Well, actually, we only have five minutes for the
35   drama, so ...

1   DRIVER 1: Anyway, thanks for stopping. I have a flat tire.

2   DRIVER 4: No problem. I have two or three of those a week. Got

3   the trick right here in my trunk. *(Digs around looking for some-*

4   *thing in her trunk and mimes pulling out an aerosol can.)*

5   Fix-a-Flat! *(Mimes filling her tire with air.)*

6   DRIVER 1: Wow! Does that stuff really work?

7   DRIVER 4: Well, like I said, I have two or three flats a week, so ...

8   probably not. But it should get you home.

9   DRIVER 1: That's all I want! Thank you so much for stopping. I

10   hope I didn't make you late for anything.

11   DRIVER 4: Nah. I was already late for a church planning meeting.

12   No trouble at all.

13   DRIVER 1: Well, thanks again. I won't forget this.

14   DRIVER 4: No problem. Have a nice evening! *(DRIVER 1 gets back*

15   *into car and drives away. DRIVER 4 gets into her car and starts*

16   *to do the same.)*

17   DRIVER 4: Where was I? Oh, that's right — serving God where

18   you are. The real trouble is, it's so hard to know what serving

19   God looks like. I'd better keep my eyes open ...

20

21

22

23

24

25

26

27

28

29

30

31

32

33

34

35

The Journey Is the Destination

A sketch about being thankful for the struggle.

Theme: Giving thanks, struggling

**Scripture
References:** 1 Timothy 6:12, 1 Thessalonians 5:18

Synopsis: One reluctant hiker sees hiking as an exercise in futility, while the other sees worth in the journey.

Cast: Hiker 1
Hiker 2

Props: Two backpacks.

Setting: A mountain.

1   *(Two HIKERS with backpacks enter either side and wander dur-*
2   *ing the sketch, going higher if they can.)*
3   **HIKER 1:** Whew! Isn't this great? There's just nothing like a
4   mountain hike to make you appreciate the beauty around us.
5   **HIKER 2:** Yeah, right. How much farther?
6   **HIKER 1:** What's wrong? If I didn't know better, I'd think you
7   weren't enjoying yourself.
8   **HIKER 2:** *(Sarcastically)* Why wouldn't I be enjoying myself? My
9   legs hurt, my back hurts, it feels like I'm carrying a bag full
10   of bricks on my back, and I have no idea where in the world
11   we're going to end up!
12   **HIKER 1:** I know! Isn't it exciting?
13   **HIKER 2:** How can you say that? This is hard!
14   **HIKER 1:** Anything worthwhile is worth the struggle. Don't you
15   think?
16   **HIKER 2:** Let's see, where have I heard that before? Oh yeah, I
17   think it was from you — about twenty-three times on this
18   hike!
19   **HIKER 1:** Oh, come on. This journey has a purpose, you know.
20   **HIKER 2:** And what exactly would that be?
21   **HIKER 1:** To get to the top, of course.
22   **HIKER 2:** And why is that so important?
23   **HIKER 1:** Oh, I think you'll see.
24   **HIKER 2:** Well, I'd better. This backpack is killing me!
25   **HIKER 1:** *(Reaching the top)* There!
26   **HIKER 2:** Wow! What a great view! You can see forever from up
27   here!
28   **HIKER 1:** Yes, you can. Isn't it beautiful? *(Sits down.)*
29   **HIKER 2:** Boy, I'll say. How did you know about this place? *(Sits*
30   *down beside HIKER 1.)*
31   **HIKER 1:** Well … I didn't — exactly.
32   **HIKER 2:** Excuse me?
33   **HIKER 1:** Nope. Just kind of followed a hunch.
34   **HIKER 2:** You mean to tell me that we started out on this trip not
35   knowing where we were going, and struggling really hard to get

1   here, and you didn't even have a clue as to where we would
2   end up?
3   HIKER 1: Pretty much. Isn't it beautiful, though?
4   HIKER 2: Well, yeah …
5   HIKER 1: And you know what?
6   HIKER 2: What?
7   HIKER 1: I'll bet you wouldn't be half as thankful for this view if
8   you hadn't had to struggle for it.
9   HIKER 2: I dunno. I think I'd take a helicopter lift up here any day
10   … and love it.
11   HIKER 1: Well, that may be. But I still think you'd appreciate it
12   more if you had to struggle to get here.
13   HIKER 2: You're probably right.
14   HIKER 1: Well, time to go. *(Rises.)*
15   HIKER 2: Excuse me?
16   HIKER 1: It's time to start heading down.
17   HIKER 2: Down? You mean like the same way we got up?
18   HIKER 1: We can't stay on the mountaintop forever.
19   HIKER 2: Who's talking forever? We just got here.
20   HIKER 1: And we need to get going. Come on. *(HIKER 1 begins the*
21   *descent.)*
22   HIKER 2: *(Pause and rises.)* Wait! Doesn't Search and Rescue have
23   a helicopter? *(Follows him down quickly.)*
24
25
26
27
28
29
30
31
32
33
34
35

Lamp-O-Rama

*A sketch about having light and
choosing to live in the darkness.*

Theme: Living in the light

**Scripture
Reference:** Ephesians 5:8-14

Synopsis: A customer who recently bought a lamp can't
seem to figure out that it needs a power source
in order to work.

Cast: Customer
Salesperson

Props: Lamp, paper, pen, coat.

Setting: A retail store specializing in lamps. In a promi-
nent place, there is a sign that says
"Lamp-O-Rama." On the flip side of the sign
are the words, "The Next Day ..." Place a
small table or desk with chair at Center Stage.

1   *(A SALESPERSON is either standing or seated at a desk. CUS-*
2   *TOMER walks in with a lamp and a frustrated look on his face.)*
3   CUSTOMER: Excuse me?
4   SALESPERSON: Yes, sir. How can I help you?
5   CUSTOMER: Well, you see, I bought this lamp yesterday …
6   SALESPERSON: Ah yes, I remember! You were having a terrible
7   time getting around your apartment at night because you
8   were always tripping over things …
9   CUSTOMER: Wow! That's right. You must not get many
10   customers in here.
11 SALESPERSON: Well, sir … I just remember the … special ones.
12   How can I help?
13 CUSTOMER: Well, this lamp you sold me doesn't work.
14 SALESPERSON: Really?
15 CUSTOMER: Yes. I put it right in the center of my apartment and
16   when it got dark, it was just as dark as it has always been.
17 SALESPERSON: Hmmm. What happened right after you plugged
18   it in?
19 CUSTOMER: Excuse me?
20 SALESPERSON: Sir, you did plug it in to the wall outlet, didn't you?
21 CUSTOMER: Uh …
22 SALESPERSON: Sir, you have to have a source of power for the
23   lamp to work.
24 CUSTOMER: OK. I'll try that. *(He exits briefly. As he does, the*
25   *SALESPERSON goes back to her desk and holds up a sign for the*
26   *audience to see that reads, "The Next Day." She then goes back*
27   *to writing something on a sheet of paper. CUSTOMER enters*
28   *again after a pause of about fifteen seconds.)* Excuse me?
29 SALESPERSON: Yes, sir. Can I help you?
30 CUSTOMER: Well, I bought a lamp a couple of days ago.
31 SALESPERSON: I remember. How did the plugging in thing go?
32 CUSTOMER: Wow. Yeah, right. Well, it still didn't work.
33 SALESPERSON: Tell me about it.
34 CUSTOMER: Well, I plugged it in, just like you said, and then
35   when it got dark, it was just as dark as before.

1   SALESPERSON: *(Trying to be patient)* **What happened when you**
2   **turned the switch?**
3   CUSTOMER: **Huh?**
4   SALESPERSON: *(Pausing for effect with head down)* **The switch.**
5   **You did turn on the switch, didn't you?**
6   CUSTOMER: **Uh ...**
7   SALESPERSON: **Here.** *(Hands CUSTOMER the paper.)* **Here are**
8   **some directions I wrote down when you left yesterday. Let me**
9   **know how it goes.**
10 CUSTOMER: *(Shrugs.)* **OK ...** *(He exits and the SALESPERSON*
11   *holds up the "Next Day" sign again. After a brief pause,*
12   *CUSTOMER enters, holding lamp.)*
13 CUSTOMER: **Excuse me? I bought a lamp here ...**
14 SALESPERSON: **Yes, sir. Did it work when you turned it on?**
15 CUSTOMER: **Wow. Uh, yeah, it did. Worked great. Lit up the**
16   **whole place.**
17 SALESPERSON: **I see. I notice you brought the lamp back.**
18 CUSTOMER: **Uh, yeah. I want to return it.**
19 SALESPERSON: **Oh? Is there a problem?**
20 CUSTOMER: **Uh, yeah. I mean, no — not with the lamp.**
21 SALESPERSON: **Then why are you wanting to return it?**
22 CUSTOMER: **Well, you see, when I turned on the lamp, I noticed**
23   **that the reason I was having a hard time getting around my**
24   **apartment was that it's a real mess!**
25 SALESPERSON: **And ...**
26 CUSTOMER: **And if I have the lamp, I'll only have to clean up the**
27   **apartment because I'll know what the problem is.**
28 SALESPERSON: **Yes?**
29 CUSTOMER: **Well ... heh-heh ...that'd be an awful lot of work ...**
30 SALESPERSON: **Sir, do you mind a little helpful advice?**
31 CUSTOMER: **No-no! Go right ahead.**
32 SALESPERSON: **Well, wouldn't it make a whole lot more sense to**
33   **clean up your apartment and keep the lamp? I mean, you're**
34   **just going to keep tripping over things and hurting yourself if**
35   **you keep stumbling over things in the dark.**

1 CUSTOMER: I have hit my head a few times …
2 SALESPERSON: *(Sarcastically)* I'm stunned. You see, it just doesn't
3   make any sense to want to stay in the darkness when every-
4   thing can be clear to you in the light, does it?
5 CUSTOMER: No, I suppose you're right. *(Pause)* OK, I'll give it a try.
6 SALESPERSON: Good for you. Have a nice day. *(She turns to get*
7   *her coat to leave as CUSTOMER heads for the exit. He stops and*
8   *turns around and notices her leaving.)*
9 CUSTOMER: Excuse me?
10 SALESPERSON: Yes?
11 CUSTOMER: You've been so helpful — can I buy you lunch?
12 SALESPERSON: Oh, you don't have to do that, sir …
13 CUSTOMER: No, really. I'd love to.
14 SALESPERSON: Well, I *am* hungry …
15 CUSTOMER: Terrific! Let's go.
16 SALESPERSON: OK. Where did you park your car? *(Both begin*
17   *walking Off-stage.)*
18 CUSTOMER: It's at my apartment.
19 SALESPERSON: Your apartment? What's it doing there?
20 CUSTOMER: Well, I just can't seem to figure out how to get it
21   to go … *(Fade as they exit.)*
22
23
24
25
26
27
28
29
30
31
32
33
34
35

Lead Us Not ...

A sketch about the reality of temptation.

Theme: Temptation

Scripture References: 1 Corinthians 7:5, 10:13, Luke 11:4

Synopsis: A dad who counsels his kids about temptations they face has some issues of his own to work out as he prepares his taxes.

Cast: Dad
Kirsten
David
Mom

Props: Pen, calculator, assorted papers and bills.

Setting: The living room of a typical American family. Place a table with two chairs at Center Stage.

1 *(DAD is sitting at the table poring over bills, getting ready to pre-*
2 *pare his taxes. KIRSTEN enters from Stage Left.)*
3 **DAD:** *(Engrossed in paperwork)* **All right, we spent four hundred**
4   **thirty-five dollars on shampoos and conditioners this year ...**
5   **that's gotta be a medical deduction ...**
6 **KIRSTEN: Hey, Dad.**
7 **DAD:** *(Into his work, looks up briefly.)* **Hey, Princess.**
8 **KIRSTEN:** *(Pause)* **Uh, Dad?**
9 **DAD:** *(Still distracted)* **Yeah?**
10 **KIRSTEN: Could I ask you a question?**
11 **DAD: Sure, honey. What's up?**
12 **KIRSTEN: Well I was wondering ...** *(Pause)*
13 **DAD: Uh-huh ...**
14 **KIRSTEN:** *(Sitting down at the table)* **You were my age once, right?**
15 **DAD:** *(Looking up, smiling sarcastically)* **Well, actually, I was born a**
16   **strapping twenty-two-year-old. It was a tough delivery, but it**
17   **saved my parents from having to pay for a lot of diapers ....**
18 **KIRSTEN: All right, all right. What I mean is, when you were a kid,**
19   **were you ever tempted to do things you knew you shouldn't?**
20 **DAD:** *(Getting interested)* **Well ... yeah. Sure I was.** *(Pause)* **Could**
21   **you be more specific?**
22 **KIRSTEN:** *(Quickly)* **Well, it's my friends. Sometimes when I'm**
23   **with them, I feel like saying and doing things that I wouldn't**
24   **with my youth group friends. You know what I mean?**
25 **DAD:** *(Pause)* **Yeah, I think so. It's sort of like being one person for**
26   **the church crowd and another for the rest of the world.**
27 **KIRSTEN: Yeah! I mean, I don't really want to do anything bad,**
28   **but I just feel like a hypocrite when I'm talking with them**
29   **sometimes. Like I'm not sure anyone would know I'm a**
30   **Christian.**
31 **DAD: Well, Kirsten, I think that you have to remember that in**
32   **everything you do, you have to be consistent with what you**
33   **believe.**
34 **KIRSTEN: But that's so hard. How do you do it at work?**
35 **DAD: Well, uh ...** *(Thinking)* **I guess before I do anything, I think**

1   about how it will affect my coworkers and if they'll see me as
2   a Christian because of it. *(Pause)* Most of the time. I mess up
3   a lot too, you know.
4   KIRSTEN: So you think it can be done?
5   DAD: Oh, sure. It's not easy. But the Bible says that we won't be
6   tempted beyond what we're able to overcome. So try to
7   remember that you can do it.
8   KIRSTEN: OK. But it's not easy, is it?
9   DAD: Not always. But it's the right thing.
10 KIRSTEN: Yeah, I guess so. Thanks Dad.
11 DAD: No problem. *(KIRSTEN exits.)* Now, let's see — where was I?
12 Oh yeah ... all right, we gave how much to Our Sisters of
13 Perpetual Poverty this year? Says here two bags of clothes.
14 *(Looking around)* Or maybe it was *(Writing in a one to change*
15 *the receipt)* ... twelve. Yeah, that's perfect! *(DAVID enters Stage*
16 *Right.)*
17 DAVID: Hey, Dad!
18 DAD: *(Looking up briefly)* Hey, Sport!
19 DAVID: Hey Dad, you gotta minute?
20 DAD: Sure, David, what's up?
21 DAVID: Well, I need your advice. You know how hard I've been
22 working in chemistry ...
23 DAD: Sure I do! You brought home an eighty-one on your last test!
24 DAVID: Well, that's just it. I don't think I really did.
25 DAD: What do you mean?
26 DAVID: Well, when we went over the tests in class, I noticed
27 several questions weren't marked wrong when they really
28 should've been. I think she skipped a whole page. I really
29 deserve a sixty-eight.
30 DAD: I see. That's a tough one.
31 DAVID: I know. I need the class, and there's no way she'll ever
32 catch it. I'm really tempted not to do anything about it. What
33 should I do?
34 DAD: Well, son, I think you know what you should do. Would you
35 really feel good about a grade you didn't earn?

1   **DAVID: Well ...** *(Pause)* **Yeah, I could live with it.**

2   **DAD: David!**

3   **DAVID: I could live with it more than I could live with failing!**

4   **DAD: David, are you serious?**

5   **DAVID: Well, I guess not. But it's really tempting.**

6   **DAD: The tough things in life are. But I think you'll make the right**

7   **choice.**

8   **DAVID: Yeah. I guess I already have. Thanks, Dad.**

9   **DAD: I'm proud of you, Son.** *(DAVID exits.)* **Now, let's see ... is**

10   **there any record at all of the money I've been making**

11   **consulting on the side? Not as far as the IRS is concerned! Ha!**

12   **That oughta save about four hundred dollars ...**

13   **MOM:** *(From Off-stage or on)* **How's it going, honey?**

14   **DAD: Just fine, dear. Should be getting a healthy refund again**

15   **this year!**

16   **MOM: That's great. I'm sure glad you do our taxes — I don't think**

17   **I'd trust anyone else.**

18   **DAD: Oh? Why's that?**

19   **MOM: Well, I was just talking to Jill and she said they got audited**

20   **last year. I guess Frank was a little less than honest on a**

21   **few things.**

22   **DAD: Oh ... really?**

23   **MOM: Yeah. I guess all those years of not being audited made him**

24   **think it would never happen to him. The temptation finally**

25   **got to him.**

26   **DAD:** *(Pause)* **You don't say.**

27   **MOM: Yeah. It cost them about three thousand dollars in penalties.**

28   **I'm just glad you're so careful and honest. You would never**

29   **do anything like that ... would you?**

30   **DAD:** *(Gathering all his papers and doing some recalculating)* **Uh ...**

31   **no, no! I wouldn't even be tempted!** *(To himself as he erases)*

32   **No medical expenses ... two bags of clothes to Our Sisters of**

33   **Perpetual Poverty ... Now how much consulting was that?**

34

35

The Least of These

A sketch on showing love to others.

Theme: Love

**Scripture
References:** John 21:15, Matthew 25:37

Synopsis: A pastor is visited by his yuppie brother, who can't understand what motivates him to work at an inner city rescue mission.

Cast: Two Homeless People (brief non-speaking parts; could be Fisher and Mary with clothing changes.)
Pastor
Janie
Nathan
Fisher
Mary

Props: Two serving spoons and two plates.

Setting: A rescue mission. There should be a bench at one side.

1   *(PASTOR is standing behind a rescue mission food line with a*
2   *helper, JANIE, and they are distributing food to the homeless.*
3   *Two HOMELESS PEOPLE, preferably wearing some rather*
4   *ragged clothes, go through the line with plates as PASTOR and*
5   *JANIE pantomime putting food on them. The third person through*
6   *the line should be NATHAN, who does not have a plate but has*
7   *come to talk to PASTOR. The PASTOR, busy cheerfully handing*
8   *out food, does not immediately recognize him.)*
9   **PASTOR: Sir, the plates are down at that end ...**
10   **NATHAN: No thanks! I've already eaten!**
11   **PASTOR: Nathan? Hey, big brother!** *(Comes out from behind the*
12   *food line to give him a hug.)* **What in the world are you doing**
13   **down here?**
14   **NATHAN: Jim! Just came down to see how my little bro is getting**
15   **along! How are you?**
16   **PASTOR: Couldn't be better! How about yourself?**
17   **NATHAN: Just dandy!** *(Pause)* **Is this a bad time?**
18   **PASTOR:** *(Looking back at JANIE)* **Janie? You think you can handle**
19   **it for a while?**
20   **JANIE: Sure, Pastor Jim. I think the rush is over.**
21   **PASTOR: Thanks!** *(Turning back to NATHAN)* **So, what's new? Oh**
22   **— come on over here and sit down.** *(They move to Downstage,*
23   *Left or Right, and sit on a bench. Before NATHAN sits down, he*
24   *brushes off the bench and then wipes his hands on his pants, as*
25   *though he is disgusted by the filthy nature of the mission.)*
26   **NATHAN: Well, not much, I guess. Still slaving away at the firm**
27   **and all. You?**
28   **PASTOR: Well, I'd like to say it's all the same, but you know, there**
29   **really aren't two days alike around here. Still, it's been really**
30   **busy, and ...** *(FISHER, a homeless man, staggers up to the PASTOR*
31   *and leans on his shoulder.)* **Hey, Fisher! What can I do for you?**
32   **FISHER: Well, I just wanted to know if there was dessert tonight!**
33   **I gotta keep up my strength, you know!**
34   **PASTOR: Oh, I know, Fisher! Hey, I'd like you to meet my brother.**
35   **This is Nathan. Nathan, this is Fisher.** *(They shake hands, but*

1   *NATHAN is very uncomfortable and wipes his hand after they are*

2   *finished shaking.)*

3   **FISHER: Pleased to make your acquaintance!**

4   **NATHAN: Same here.**

5   **FISHER: Know why they call me Fisher?**

6   **NATHAN:** *(Awkward brief pause)* **Why?**

7   **FISHER: I used to work as a bricklayer!** *(Pause, as NATHAN is try-*

8   *ing to figure out why this would mean he was called Fisher. He*

9   *waits for an explanation that never comes.)* **So, what line of work**

10   **you in?**

11   **NATHAN: Uh ... I'm ... uh ... I'm a lawyer.**

12   **FISHER: Oh, yeah? Me, too. In fact, I got a big case tomorrow. You**

13   **think we're gonna have dessert tonight or not, Reverend? I**

14   **need my strength ...**

15   **PASTOR: I think Janie's got some Twinkies up there, Fisher. Help**

16   **yourself.**

17   **FISHER: Don't mind if I do!** *(To NATHAN)* **You want one?**

18   **NATHAN: No. No thanks.**

19   **FISHER:** *(To PASTOR)* **Hey, Reverend? You think I could ...**

20   **PASTOR: You can have Nathan's twinkie too, Fisher.** *(FISHER*

21   *walks off.)* **He's a character.**

22   **NATHAN: I'll say. Why exactly** *do* **they call him Fisher?**

23   **PASTOR: I have no idea. So, what brings you down here?**

24   **NATHAN: Oh, no reason. Just thought I'd see how you're**

25   **getting along.**

26   **PASTOR:** *(Suspiciously)* **Uh-huh.**

27   **NATHAN: What?**

28   **PASTOR: It's Mom, isn't it? She sent you down here again,**

29   **didn't she?**

30   **NATHAN: What? No!** *(Pause)* **Well, she may have said it would be**

31   **nice if I'd check and see how things are going, but I'd hardly**

32   **say that was sending me ...**

33   **PASTOR: And to try and talk me into taking that pastorate on the**

34   **upper west side, right?**

35   **NATHAN: No! Is there a pastorate opening there?**

1   PASTOR: Nathan, you have always been a good liar. And a good
2   lawyer, too. Funny how that works …
3   NATHAN: Watch it, watch it. *(Pause)* All right, she may have men-
4   tioned the opening in Cloverdale.
5   PASTOR: Did she also mention that I told her I had no intention of
6   applying there?
7   NATHAN: Well, she mentioned that, yes …
8   PASTOR: In spite of her attempts to apply on my behalf …
9   NATHAN: Like?
10   PASTOR: Like making up posters of me with a resume attached
11   and nailing them to the church door like Luther's Theses …
12   NATHAN: She did not!
13   PASTOR: I wouldn't put it past her.
14   NATHAN: Oh, come on, Jim. She just wants the best for you,
15   you know?
16   PASTOR: And what makes her think … or you too, for that matter
17   … that what's best for me isn't right here?
18   NATHAN: Well … *(Pause as he looks around)* would you like a list,
19   or shall I keep it short?
20   PASTOR: Nathan, this is my place! This is where I belong! *(Just
21   then, a homeless woman, MARY, comes up to him.)* Hey, Mary!
22   What's up?
23   MARY: Sorry to bother you, Pastor, but I was wondering if you
24   could help me with my foot again.
25   PASTOR: Did the bandage come loose again?
26   MARY: Yes. I walked a few too many miles today! But I think it was
27   worth it — I think I got a job down at the flea market on
28   fourth.
29   PASTOR: Wow! That's great, Mary! Sure — I'll help you fix that
30   up again in just a few minutes, OK?
31   MARY: Thanks again, Pastor. Sorry to interrupt! *(She walks off.)*
32   PASTOR: No problem, Mary. *(To NATHAN)* Now, what were we
33   saying?
34   NATHAN: I just wonder if you couldn't be just as useful at the
35   church on the west side, that's all.

1 PASTOR: That's not really the question, though. You know how
2   God talks about feeding his sheep and loving the least of
3   these? For me, that's here.
4 NATHAN: How do you know?
5 PASTOR: *(Laughs.)* When you seek to be in the center of his will,
6   you know! I can't explain it any better than that. Look. When
7   you go back to talk to Mom, tell her I'm where God wants me
8   to be. The same thing I've been telling her ever since she put
9   my picture on milk cartons all over the city.
10 NATHAN: You really think you're getting through to any of these
11   people?
12 PASTOR: I'm feeding his sheep. That's my job. And yours. To show
13   God's love wherever we are.
14 NATHAN: Gosh, Jim. I just hope you know what you're doing
15   down here.
16 PASTOR: I do. I'm feeding, clothing, and visiting his sheep. And
17   when I do that, Jesus says, I do it for him.
18 NATHAN: I guess. *(He rises to leave.)* OK. I'll tell Mom you're
19   doing all right down here. But I wouldn't hold out for her to
20   visit. She gets scared when one of those famine commercials
21   comes on TV late at night!
22 PASTOR: That's OK. I'll still visit her as always. Thanks though,
23   Nathan.
24 NATHAN: Sure. You take care, OK?
25 PASTOR: You bet. You too.
26 NATHAN: *(Starts to exit but as he does, he stops, looks around, and*
27   *shakes his head. To PASTOR)* You know, I wouldn't do what
28   you're doing for all the money in the world. *(He exits.)*
29 PASTOR: *(Laughs and looks around.)* Funny. *(Pause)* Neither
30   would I ... *(Exits.)*
31
32
33
34
35

Leftovers Again?

A sketch on respecting God's earth.

Theme:	Earth Day, God's creation
Scripture Reference:	Psalm 33:5
Synopsis:	A church potluck leads to the realization that we can all become more earth conscious than we already are.
Cast:	Luke Warmer Mead E. Ocre Wiebe Wasteful Ima Zealot
Props:	Church bulletin; plates, napkins, glasses, and eating utensils (or these may be mimed); tuna can.
Setting:	A church fellowship hall, where a potluck dinner is in progress. A long table should be placed at Center Stage with four chairs.

1   (*LUKE WARMER, MEADE E. OCRE, WIEBE WASTEFUL, and*
2   *IMA ZEALOT sit at the table and pantomime eating.*)
3   **LUKE WARMER: Isn't this great?! I love church potlucks.**
4   **MEAD E. OCRE: You bet! What did you bring?**
5   **LUKE WARMER: Uh ... I love church potlucks. How about you, Ima?**
6   **IMA ZEALOT: Oh, I don't know. Everyone covers things with**
7   **aluminum foil ...**
8   **WIEBE WASTEFUL: And this bothers you because ...**
9   **IMA ZEALOT: Well, have you ever seen any recycle bins at a**
10   **potluck?**
11   **LUKE WARMER: So that was you who put "Save the Trees"**
12   **posters all over the church?**
13   **IMA ZEALOT: On recycled paper ...**
14   **WIEBE WASTEFUL: I don't see what difference our little church**
15   **could make.**
16   **MEAD E. OCRE: I recycle. In fact, I don't even read the newspapers**
17   **before I put them in the recycle bin.**
18   **IMA ZEALOT: But that's not right either! You shouldn't subscribe**
19   **to the paper if you don't read it!**
20   **MEAD E. OCRE: Then what would I recycle?**
21   **LUKE WARMER: Look — I think Wiebe is right. Why recycle?**
22   **IMA ZEALOT: Psalm 33:5 says, "The earth is full of the goodness**
23   **of the Lord" (KJV).**
24   **WIEBE WASTEFUL: Ha! Well, the psalmist never visited Las Vegas!**
25   **IMA ZEALOT: Seriously, David said, "The earth is the Lord's, and**
26   **the fullness thereof ..." (Psalm 24:1, KJV). We have a respon-**
27   **sibility to take care of it.**
28   **MEAD E. OCRE: Well, I don't leave anything *to* recycle. This is**
29   **great tuna salad, Wiebe!**
30   **WIEBE WASTEFUL: Thanks!**
31   **IMA ZEALOT: Was it made with dolphin-safe tuna?**
32   **WIEBE WASTEFUL: I don't know. No dolphins showed up to**
33   **protest ...**
34   **IMA ZEALOT: I'm serious! What are we doing as a church to help**
35   **the environment?**

1   WIEBE WASTEFUL: Well, it says here in the bulletin that we're
2   hosting a paper drive.
3   MEAD E. OCRE: I've got a bunch ... new, even.
4   IMA ZEALOT: *(After grabbing bulletin)* But look — this bulletin
5   isn't even printed on recyclable paper. Do we really care?
6   WIEBE and MEAD E. OCRE: *(Shrugging shoulders)* No.
7   LUKE WARMER: Well, I do. From now on, I'm gonna recycle
8   everything! *(Holds up tuna can.)* Starting with this can!
9   IMA ZEALOT: Way to go, Luke! I wish more men would have that
10   attitude!
11   MEAD E. OCRE: *(Pause)* You mean Mormons don't recycle either?
12   IMA ZEALOT: What?
13   MEAD E. OCRE: You said you wished that Mormons recycled.
14   IMA ZEALOT: That's not what I said. I meant humanity in general.
15   MEAD E. OCRE: I know they don't drink coffee. ...
16   IMA ZEALOT: No, no, no. I just think that recycling is so impor-
17   tant, everyone should do it.
18   MEAD E. OCRE: But why does it have to be the Mormons?
19   IMA ZEALOT: It doesn't! Just recycle! *(She storms off.)*
20   MEAD E. OCRE: Man, there are some people you just can't talk
21   religion with ...
22
23
24
25
26
27
28
29
30
31
32
33
34
35

Never Alone

A sketch on showing God's comfort.

Theme: Compassion, friendship, comfort, fear

**Scripture
References:** 2 Corinthians 1:3-4, Galatians 6:1-5

Synopsis: After Amy is devastated by the break-up of a relationship, Beth consoles her with a reminder of God's constant love.

Cast: Amy
Beth

Props: None.

Setting: Some steps outside a school. Use the chancel steps, if visible to the audience. Otherwise, use chairs.

1   (*AMY sits on the steps, sobbing audibly. BETH enters.*)
2   **BETH: Hey, Amy. Are you all right?**
3   **AMY: Oh, hi, Beth. Sure. I'm fine.**
4   **BETH: Why were you crying like that?**
5   **AMY:** *(Pause)* **Well, how am I supposed to cry?**
6   **BETH: No, no. I just wondered why you were crying in the**
7   **first place.**
8   **AMY: Oh, no reason. I'm fine ...** *(Begins sobbing again.)*
9   **BETH: That was really convincing. What's wrong?**
10   **AMY: Oh, I'm sorry. It's Brad.**
11   **BETH: Your boyfriend?**
12   **AMY: Well, not anymore ...**
13   **BETH:** *(Sitting beside AMY)* **Oh Amy! I'm sorry.**
14   **AMY: Yeah, me too.**
15   **BETH: What happened?**
16   **AMY: Oh, nothing really. We had too much in common.**
17   **BETH: How do you mean?**
18   **AMY: Well, I thought he was wonderful. Apparently, so did he.**
19   **BETH: Oh. Well, better that you find out now, right?**
20   **AMY: As opposed to after we lived happily ever after?**
21   **BETH: You know what I mean.**
22   **AMY: I suppose so. It's just that I have never felt so ... alone.**
23   **BETH: You're not alone.**
24   **AMY: Thanks. You want to spend the rest of your life with me?**
25   **BETH:** *(Laughing just a little)* **No. I'm not talking about me. Have**
26   **you tried praying about it?**
27   **AMY: What? Why would I do that?**
28   **BETH: Why wouldn't you? God really cares about you, and he**
29   **doesn't want to see you hurting.**
30   **AMY: I don't know. It's not like Brad and I just went to Sunday**
31   **school together. I know there were areas of our relationship**
32   **that God wouldn't necessarily approve of.**
33   **BETH: So?**
34   **AMY: So why would he want me to talk to him about it?**
35   **BETH: Because he cares about you.**

1   AMY: *(Pause)* I don't know. I'm not sure I've made God much of a
2   priority. Why would I be one to him?
3   BETH: I don't know. Why would any of us? But strangely enough,
4   we are.
5   AMY: You really think I should pray about this?
6   BETH: Amy, God is really the only one who can give you the kind
7   of comfort you need right now. If you don't ask him for it,
8   you'll just keep feeling alone.
9   AMY: *(Pause)* You really think it will help?
10   BETH: I know it will. It always does.
11   AMY: Gee. Thanks, Beth. I still feel miserable, but I'm starting to
12   think it's not the end of the world.
13   BETH: Of course not, Amy. You'll make it.
14   AMY: I guess you're right. I'm starting to feel better already.
15   BETH: See? You'll never be alone as long as you believe. And as
16   long as you've got me for a friend.
17   AMY: *(As they both rise)* I guess so! You know, you're pretty good at
18   this ... "friend" thing.
19   BETH: Well, if you must know, all my aptitude tests said that I
20   should seek out being a friend as a career goal.
21   AMY: Really?
22   BETH: Yup. *(As they start to walk off together)* Well, actually, that
23   was number two.
24   AMY: Oh? And what was number one?
25   BETH: Dinosaur trainer.
26   AMY: But there aren't any ...
27   BETH: Well, it's a good thing I have this to fall back on then, huh?
28   AMY: For you and me both ...
29
30
31
32
33
34
35

On Second Thought...

A sketch on doing what we say we will do.

Theme: Obedience

**Scripture
References:** Matthew 21:28-32, James 1:22

Synopsis: A parachutist claims he will check his chute,
but he doesn't. His first jump could also be his
last!

Cast: Sergeant
Johnson
Smith

Props: Magazine.

Setting: A parachute jump training facility. Place a
bench (or small church pew or row of chairs)
at Center Stage.

1   *(A drill SERGEANT gives last-minute instructions to a pair of*
2   *first-time jumpers, JOHNSON and SMITH, at Center Stage.)*
3   SERGEANT: OK, men, you've gone through all the training. I have
4   no doubt that you'll be able to get out of the plane, pull the
5   ripcord, and land properly. There's just one more thing, and
6   it's very important.
7   JOHNSON: What's that, Sarge?
8   SERGEANT: That parachute is the only thing between you and
9   instant death. Make sure that you take the time to unpack it
10   and check it thoroughly before you get into that plane.
11   SMITH: But Sarge — those chutes are packed by someone who
12   knows what they're doing, right?
13   SERGEANT: Of course. They've packed thousands of chutes.
14   SMITH: So why undo all their work and make tons more of it for
15   ourselves?
16   JOHNSON: I'll take the time. I know how important it is to you, sir!
17   SERGEANT: It's important to *you*, Johnson. It's a safeguard. You
18   want to make sure it's going to open properly, right?
19   JOHNSON: I'll double-check mine, sir! Triple-check it, even!
20   SERGEANT: Good, Johnson. You guys know how a chute should
21   look. After you take it apart, repack it correctly — just to
22   make sure it's safe.
23   SMITH: Sir, I just don't see that it's necessary. That would take
24   another half-hour.
25   SERGEANT: Better than taking your life, eh, Smith?
26   SMITH: Yes, but these guys …
27   JOHNSON: I'll get on it right away, sir. Can't be too safe, I always
28   say.
29   SERGEANT: *(A little annoyed with his "yes - man" technique)* Yes.
30   Well, the plane leaves in an hour, so you'd better get packing.
31   Or repacking, as it were. Ha-ha! *(Exits.)*
32   JOHNSON: Yes sir, you can count on me! I'll pack it four or five
33   times to be safe! *(He calls to him as he leaves, but as soon as*
34   *he is out of earshot, he goes back over to his seat, pulls out a*
35   *magazine, and starts to read.)*

1   SMITH: Well?

2   JOHNSON: Well, what?

3   SMITH: Aren't you going to start repacking your chute, Mr. "I'll

4   do it four or five times" brown-noser?

5   JOHNSON: Are you kidding? I wouldn't undo that chute to save

6   my life. *(Realizes what he is saying and chuckles to himself.)*

7   Pardon the expression.

8   SMITH: But you said ...

9   JOHNSON: Look. You were right. Those guys that pack them know

10   what they're doing. And besides, I'm not into wasting my time.

11   SMITH: I don't know. He has a point about it being the last thing

12   between us and the ground. Do you really want to put that in

13   someone else's hands?

14   JOHNSON: To save a half-hour, I do.

15   SMITH: Then why did you tell the Sarge that you would?

16   JOHNSON: *(Laughing)* It's what he wanted to hear! You've got a lot

17   to learn about this man's army.

18   SMITH: Maybe. All the same, I think I'm going to go unpack and

19   repack my chute. I'll see you at the plane. *(Exits with JOHN-*

20   *SON following)*

21   JOHNSON: Suit yourself. But you're wasting your time ... *(Both*

22   *JOHNSON and SMITH re-enter, pantomiming carrying para-*

23   *chutes. They sit down on the bench as if they are on an airplane,*

24   *about to jump. Characters will have to talk loudly, as if to be*

25   *heard over the roar of the engines.)*

26   SERGEANT: *(From Off-stage)* One minute to drop zone!

27   JOHNSON: So, was your chute OK?

28   SMITH: Yeah, it was fine. Packed like it was brand-new.

29   JOHNSON: I told you you were wasting your time.

30   SMITH: Maybe so. But I feel pretty good about the jump. At least

31   I know everything's going to go well. Are you all set?

32   JOHNSON: I feel fine.

33   SMITH: I mean, did you check your chute?

34   JOHNSON: Why bother? Yours was fine, wasn't it?

35   SMITH: Yeah, but ...

1   **SERGEANT: Time to go!**

2   **JOHNSON:** *(Pretends to put goggles on.)* **Well, here goes NOTHING!**

3   *(Jumps Off-stage.)*

4   **SMITH: I hope so. GERONIMO!** *(Jumps.)*

5   **JOHNSON:** *(Pause)* **Uh-oh!**

6

7

8

9

10

11

12

13

14

15

16

17

18

19

20

21

22

23

24

25

26

27

28

29

30

31

32

33

34

35

One Thin Dime

A sketch on tithing.

Theme: Tithing, giving

Scripture References: 2 Corinthians 9:7, Leviticus 27:32-33

Synopsis: When Blake invites his accountant to church to figure out his ten percent tithe to the penny, his friend reminds him that God loves a cheerful giver.

Cast: Man
Accountant
Friend

Props: Adding machine, two checkbooks, two pens, offering plate.

Setting: A church service. Place a church pew (or use a row of chairs) at Center Stage.

1   *(A MAN sits on a church pew with his ACCOUNTANT and a*
2   *FRIEND. The ACCOUNTANT has a calculator or an adding*
3   *machine* [Preferred] *on which he is doing calculations throughout*
4   *the sketch.)*
5   **MAN: Listen, Miles, I don't mean to rush you, but the offering plate**
6   **has begun its rounds and I don't want to have to hold it up.**
7   **Again.**
8   **ACCOUNTANT: Patience, patience. After all, you want to get it**
9   **right down to the penny, don't you?**
10   **MAN: Well, yes, of course ... but I don't want to make anybody wait.**
11   **ACCOUNTANT: Do you want this done, or do you want it done**
12   **right?**
13   **MAN: Sorry.**
14   **FRIEND: Hey, Blake. How're you doing?**
15   **MAN: Oh, hey Andrew. Great.**
16   **FRIEND: Who's your friend? I've seen him here the last few**
17   **weeks, but ...**
18   **MAN: Friend?** *(Glancing at ACCOUNTANT)* **Oh, you mean Miles?**
19   *(Chuckles.)* **He's no friend. He's my accountant.**
20   **FRIEND: Oh. You invited your accountant to church! That's a**
21   **great idea! Jesus seemed to have a soft spot for those tax-**
22   **collector types ...**
23   **MAN:** *(Chuckles.)* **Yes, I suppose he did. But I didn't really invite**
24   **Miles to church.**
25   **FRIEND: No?**
26   **MAN: Nah. He's on retainer.**
27   **FRIEND: What?**
28   **MAN: You know. He's working for me. Got him trying to figure up**
29   **what my tithe should be right now.**
30   **FRIEND: You what? He's trying to figure up your tithe?**
31   **MAN: Yup.** *(Turning to ACCOUNTANT)* **You just about got it? The**
32   **plate's just five rows up.**
33   **ACCOUNTANT:** *(Shoots him a dirty look.)* **Almost, Mr. Stevens. Just**
34   **working on your IRA deduction.**
35   **FRIEND: IRA deduction? Look, Blake, it's probably none of my**

1   business, but wouldn't it be easier just to give ten percent?
2   MAN: Oh, but I do. That's what I pay Miles to figure out for me.
3   Ten percent.
4   FRIEND: Uh, Blake? Isn't it just a matter of moving the decimal
5   point over one place to the left?
6   MAN: Oh, I wish it were, Andrew. But nowadays there's just too
7   much room for interpretation. I'm not taking any chances.
8   FRIEND: Blake, what are you talking about?
9   MAN: Well, ten percent is ten percent. But ten percent of what? I
10   may make three thousand dollars a month, but how much do
11   I tithe?
12   FRIEND: Three hundred?
13   MAN: That's the way I used to think! But then I figured out, "Hey!
14   After federal and state taxes, I only clear two thousand dollars
15   a month.
16   FRIEND: Well, yeah, but …
17   MAN: And then there's insurance. And my tax-sheltered annuities.
18   Then my cafeteria plan and my IRA. Not to mention my auto-
19   matic payment system at my bank. I'm lucky if I see half of
20   that three thousand dollars!
21   FRIEND: But don't you think that …
22   MAN: And if I give three hundred dollars of that to the church, I'm
23   tithing more than twenty percent!
24   FRIEND: I don't think that's what the Bible says about …
25   MAN: So the way I've got it figured, I'm gonna save thousands of
26   dollars in tithes that I don't owe by having Miles here do the
27   figuring for me before the plate is passed! And he only charges
28   me forty-five dollars an hour! *(Turning to ACCOUNTANT)* It's
29   just two rows away, Miles. We gonna make it?
30   ACCOUNTANT: *(Not looking up)* Almost there …
31   MAN: Anyway, on top of it all, Miles found me a way to reclaim more
32   than half of what I'm giving in my charitable contribution
33   deduction at the end of the year! The way I figure it, I'll be
34   able to tithe without even feeling it!
35   FRIEND: Yeah. I bet you will.

1   MAN: What's that supposed to mean?

2   FRIEND: Look, Blake, I think you're missing the boat on tithing.

3   First of all, the Bible talks about giving your first fruits back

4   to God — not what's left over when Miles here gets done.

5   MAN: Look, I'm giving my ten percent!

6   FRIEND: I don't think God cares if you're giving fifty percent.

7   *(At this, the ACCOUNTANT shoots FRIEND a dirty look and*

8   *shudders. FRIEND pauses.)* Look, it's all about attitude. You

9   should want to give your ten percent joyfully because you're

10   thankful for all that God has allowed you to do and be.

11   MAN: I don't have a problem with that! I just don't want to

12   give more!

13   FRIEND: You still don't get it! You have to want to give your money

14   back to God because he's the reason you have it in the first

15   place.

16   MAN: Shhh! The plate's coming! What's the damage, Miles?

17   ACCOUNTANT: Looks like exactly forty-nine dollars and eighty-

18   seven cents.

19   MAN: Well, OK. Fifty even. *(Writes the check as FRIEND drops his*

20   *check in the plate that passes, then drops his in the plate and turns*

21   *to FRIEND.)* You happy?

22   FRIEND: Are you?

23   MAN: *(Pause)* Strangely enough … no. *(Pause)* Why do you suppose

24   that is, Andrew?

25   FRIEND: Blake, the whole purpose of tithing is that God gives us

26   the opportunity to make a sacrifice of love to him. Without

27   that attitude, you might as well not even tithe, because it's not

28   making a difference to you.

29   MAN: Hmmm. You know, you're right. I don't feel very fulfilled.

30   FRIEND: Of course not. You're tithing with your head and not your

31   heart.

32   MAN: *(Pause)* You're right. Well, not anymore! Starting right now,

33   I'm tithing the way I used to.

34   FRIEND: That's the spirit!

35   MAN: And I'm starting with the fee I was going to give Miles for the

1 **next month.** *(Writes a check as ACCOUNTANT, who was*
2 *engrossed in his calculator, slowly raises his head to look at the*
3 *audience. Pause for laughter.)*
4 **FRIEND: I'm sure that's going to make you a lot happier.**
5 **MAN:** *(Tears out check and looks up.)* **You know, it does! Come with**
6 **me to drop this in the plate.**
7 **FRIEND: Sure! It makes me feel better just to see how your**
8 **attitude has changed.** *(They rise to leave and exit, leaving the*
9 *ACCOUNTANT sitting by himself.)*
10 **ACCOUNTANT:** *(Pause, as he looks perplexed)* **How come I don't**
11 **feel any more fulfilled?**
12
13
14
15
16
17
18
19
20
21
22
23
24
25
26
27
28
29
30
31
32
33
34
35

Peerless Talent Agency

A sketch about using your talents.

Theme: Talents

Scripture Reference: Luke 19:11

Synopsis: Mr. Peerless won't let any of the actors affiliated with his agency work for fear that they'll fail, and then he won't be able to market them as the best in the business.

Cast: Receptionist
Producer
Mr. Peerless

Props: Two phones, assorted pens and papers.

Setting: The Peerless Talent Agency. There is a desk at Stage Right with an extra chair nearby and a desk at Stage Left.

1   *(RECEPTIONIST is answering calls at the desk at Stage Right.*
2   *PRODUCER sits in the nearby chair. Stage Left is another desk*
3   *with MR. PEERLESS sitting at it, looking rather not busy.)*
4   RECEPTIONIST: *(Very cheerily)* **Peerless Talent Agency, how may**
5   **I direct your call?** *(Pause)* **Yes, we have wedding singers. In**
6   **fact, they're the best singers in the world.** *(Pause)* **No, I'm**
7   **sorry — right now, none of them are choosing to sing. Sorry!**
8   **Bye-bye!**
9   RECEPTIONIST: *(As PRODUCER approaches the desk)* **May I help**
10   **you, sir?**
11   PRODUCER: **Yes. I'm the producer at the local community theater,**
12   **and I've been hearing good things about a lot of the people**
13   **you represent.**
14   RECEPTIONIST: **Yes, sir! We have the most talented musicians,**
15   **actors, dancers, and electricians in the world.**
16   PRODUCER: **Yes, well I …** *(Pause)* **Electricians?**
17   RECEPTIONIST: **Very talented electricians. Shocking, really.**
18   *(Pause)* **They're really an undervalued group.**
19   PRODUCER: **Yes, I suppose they would be.** *(Pause)* **Anyway, as I**
20   **was saying, I am producing a play, and one of my actors has**
21   **come down with laryngitis. I'm looking for someone who**
22   **could come in and take his place for this production.**
23   RECEPTIONIST: **Oooooh! I bet you are! Sorry — there's nothing**
24   **we can do.**
25   PRODUCER: **Pardon?**
26   RECEPTIONIST: **Sorry we can't help you.**
27   PRODUCER: **You don't have any actors?**
28   RECEPTIONIST: *(Laughing)* **No actors? Oh, no sir. We have plenty**
29   **of actors. In fact, we have the most talented actors in the world.**
30   PRODUCER: **Then why can't you help me?**
31   RECEPTIONIST: **Oh, I'm flattered, sir, but I can't act to save**
32   **my life!**
33   PRODUCER: **No, no. Not you! Your agency!**
34   RECEPTIONIST: **Oh! Well, none of our actors are currently**
35   **working.**

1 PRODUCER: You mean they're all busy working other jobs right
2   now, right?
3 RECEPTIONIST: They are? *(Pause)* Oh, my! If they're working
4   and Mr. Peerless didn't authorize it, I'm afraid someone is in
5   trouble!
6 PRODUCER: No, no! I'm asking ... *(Pause)* Look. Could I talk to
7   Mr. Peerless?
8 RECEPTIONIST: Sure! *(Picks up phone.)* Mr. Peerless? There's a
9   gentleman here to see you!
10 MR. PEERLESS: *(Acts as though he's waking up.)* Uh ... Send him in!
11 RECEPTIONIST: Mr. Peerless will see you now! *(Pause)* Oh, and
12   tell him about all of our actors working other jobs — he needs
13   to know that!
14 PRODUCER: But all the act ... *(Pause)* Thanks! I'll do that.
15 MR. PEERLESS: Come in, come in! What can I do for you?
16 PRODUCER: Well, I was just talking to your receptionist out there,
17   because I'm looking for an actor for my play. But she said that
18   none of your actors are working right now. Is that true?
19 MR. PEERLESS: That is true.
20 PRODUCER: So could one of them work for me?
21 MR. PEERLESS: I don't think so.
22 PRODUCER: Why not? I thought this was a talent agency!
23 MR. PEERLESS: Oh, it is! We have the finest actors, musicians,
24   writers, and carpenters in all the world.
25 PRODUCER: Yes, I've heard ... *(Pause)* carpenters ?
26 MR. PEERLESS: : Very talented carpenters. Good with construc-
27   tive criticism. *(Pause)* They're really an undervalued group.
28 PRODUCER: I'm sure. It's just that you don't usually think of
29   going to a talent agency for a carpenter.
30 MR. PEERLESS: You know how hard it is to find a good carpenter
31   nowadays? I'd think of looking everywhere.
32 PRODUCER: Anyway, that's not what I came to talk to you about.
33   I need actors. Do you have any or not?
34 MR. PEERLESS: We have some of the finest ...
35 PRODUCER: Finest actors in the world — yes, I know! Can one of

1   them star in my play?
2   MR. PEERLESS: I'm afraid not.
3   PRODUCER: Why not?
4   MR. PEERLESS: Well, you don't think I'd risk the fragile egos of
5   my performers by having them perform and possibly fail,
6   do you?
7   PRODUCER: What?
8   MR. PEERLESS: Our performers don't ever fail. That's why
9   they're the best in the world!
10   PRODUCER: But they never perform?
11   MR. PEERLESS: Nope. Well, occasionally the carpenters and
12   electricians, but ...
13   PRODUCER: Let me get this straight. You don't want your clients
14   to fail.
15   MR. PEERLESS: Right.
16   PRODUCER: So you don't ever let them perform.
17   MR. PEERLESS: Exactly.
18   PRODUCER: So even though they may be the best, no one ever
19   hears them succeed.
20   MR. PEERLESS: Or fail. That's the idea.
21   PRODUCER: But you can't possibly make any money.
22   MR. PEERLESS: That's a problem, yes.
23   PRODUCER: Can I give you a little friendly advice?
24   MR. PEERLESS: Sure.
25   PRODUCER: If you never let your performers show their talents,
26   they'll never succeed, and you won't make any money.
27   MR. PEERLESS: But they might fail. And then we couldn't boast
28   having ...
29   PRODUCER: The best talent in the world. I know. But if you don't
30   let them share their talents, you won't be in business that long.
31   And who knows? They still might be the best.
32   MR. PEERLESS: Wouldn't that be something?! *(Pause)* You know,
33   I think you might have something here!
34   PRODUCER: Of course I do! If you have talent and you don't do
35   anything with it, you might as well not have any.

1 MR. PEERLESS: Well, we do. I'll tell you what. I'll set you up with
2   the best actor in the world.
3 PRODUCER: Well, I don't really need that. I just need someone
4   who's not afraid to try.
5 MR. PEERLESS: You got it. *(Picks up phone and presses his recep-*
6   *tionist button.)* Millie? Get Bob DeNiro on the phone and tell
7   him we've got work for him.
8 RECEPTIONIST: Didn't that gentleman tell you? All our people
9   are already working!
10 MR. PEERLESS: *(Turning to PRODUCER)* What is she ...?
11 PRODUCER: Long story. Anyway, you have Robert DeNiro as
12   a client?
13 MR. PEERLESS: No, Bob DeNiro. He runs a deli over on Fourth
14   Street. But he's a great actor, too.
15 PRODUCER: I'll take him.
16 MR. PEERLESS: *(Back to RECEPTIONIST)* Just get Bob on the
17   phone and tell him to get over here as soon as possible. *(Pause,*
18   *then back to RECEPTIONIST)* Oh, and have him bring me a
19   pastrami on rye while he's at it. *(Back to PRODUCER)* Just
20   think, this could be our first break!
21 PRODUCER: I hope so. Thanks a lot.
22 MR. PEERLESS: You bet! Anything else I can do for you?
23 PRODUCER: That ought to do it. Wait a minute! There is one thing.
24 MR. PEERLESS: Name it!
25 PRODUCER: You wouldn't happen to know where I could find a
26   talented plumber, would you?
27 MR. PEERLESS: Are you kidding? You know how hard it is to find
28   a good plumber these days?
29
30
31
32
33
34
35

The Phone Tree

A sketch about communication within the church.

Theme: Communication

**Scripture
Reference:**   Colossians 4:6

Synopsis: This take-off on the children's game of "telephone" features five characters, who call one another about an upcoming church service. The service has taken on some very interesting proportions by the time the last person has been called. Communication *must* be interactive in order to be effective!

Cast: Lois
Jan
Mark
Mary
Susan

Props: Five sheets of paper (phone trees), five phones (or the phones may be mimed).

Setting: The homes of five people. Place five stools across the stage.

1   *(LOIS, JAN, MARK, MARY and SUSAN sit on their stools. All sit*
2   *with their backs to the audience except LOIS. LOIS dials number*
3   *rather unexcitedly, then pauses appropriately. JAN turns around.)*
4   **JAN: Hello?**
5   **LOIS: Hi, Jan, this is Lois. How's it going?**
6   **JAN: Hey, Lois. Not too badly. What's up?**
7   **LOIS: Well, as you know, I'm on the worship committee, and —**
8   **JAN: You know, I'm just so busy — I really think I'm overcommitted**
9   **as it is —**
10   **LOIS: No, no — it's nothing like that.** *(Insert pastor's name)* **just**
11   **thought it would be a good idea to start the phone tree to let**
12   **everyone know to be in church this Sunday — the sermon is**
13   **going to be on communication.**
14   **JAN: Oh, of course. I didn't mean that I wouldn't do ... whatever**
15   **the worship committee wanted — I was ... I was talking to my**
16   **kids.** *(Aside, very clearly and slowly)* ***Kids, I would love to play***
17   ***Bible Trivia right now, but I'm busy on the phone!*** **Now, what**
18   **was it you were saying?**
19   **LOIS: Yes, well, I was saying that** *(Insert pastor's name)* **is speaking**
20   **on communication this week, and he thought it would be a**
21   **good idea if we communicated that to each other using the**
22   **phone tree — you know, to make sure everyone would be**
23   **there.**
24   **JAN: Oh, well, you know we'll be there. Did someone say we**
25   **weren't planning on being there?**
26   **LOIS: No, no. It's just that I'm right above you on the tree, and**
27   *(Looking at the tree)* **... Mark is right below you. So you** *will*
28   **call Mark?**
29   **JAN: Oh, of course! I'll do whatever is expected of me. Uh ... now**
30   **what exactly did you want me to tell him?**
31   **LOIS:** *(Sighs.)* **Tell him that you're calling on the phone tree to let**
32   **him know that the message is on communication next week.**
33   **And that he needs to call the next person on the list. OK?**
34   **JAN: Oh, yeah — sure! I can do that. Uh ... what list?**
35   **LOIS: The phone tree!**

1 JAN: Oh, yes. I'm sorry — the kids are kind of noisy today. I
2   couldn't hear you.
3 LOIS: That's fine. So you'll call Mark?
4 JAN: Of course. Right away.
5 LOIS: OK, then. We'll see you on Sunday!
6 JAN: OK, bye-bye! *(They hang up. LOIS turns around, with her back*
7   *to the audience. JAN immediately looks on her list for MARK's*
8   *number and dials it. MARK faces front.)*
9 MARK: Hello?
10 JAN: Hi, Mark! This is Jan. How're you doing?
11 MARK: Oh, hi, Jan! I'm great, how're you?
12 JAN: Just great. Listen, I'm calling on the phone tree to let you
13   know about the message next Sunday.
14 MARK: Oh?
15 JAN: Yeah … uh … *(Thinking)* Oh, yes! *(Insert pastor's name)* wanted
16   everyone to be there next week because he's talking on
17   communications.
18 MARK: Communications? You mean like radio and television?
19 JAN: Uh, yeah, I guess so. Lois wasn't that specific.
20 MARK: Oh! You know, I'll bet it's on how television is really
21   corrupting the church. I just read and article in *Church News*
22   about the same thing. And you know pastors — once a topic
23   starts making the rounds, they beat it to death …
24 JAN: You're probably right. Anyway, you'll call … *(Looking at*
25   *paper)* Mary?
26 MARK: Sure. Hey, are you going to be at Bible study on Wednesday?
27 JAN: Uh … probably not. I think Rachel's got something going on
28   at school.
29 MARK: In the summer?
30 JAN: Uh, yeah … it's some kind of … enrichment program … or
31   something …
32 MARK: OK — well, we'll see you on Sunday then?
33 JAN: Sunday? Oh, yes — of course we'll be there. Did someone say
34   that we wouldn't?
35 MARK: No, no. We'll just see you then.

1   JAN: Of course. Bye now.

2   MARK: Bye! *(JAN turns around. MARK hangs up and dials the next*

3   *number. MARY faces front.)*

4   MARY: Hello?

5   MARK: Hi, Mary? This is Mark from church.

6   MARY: Oh hi, Mark.

7   MARK: Hello. The reason I'm calling is that *(Insert pastor's name)*

8   Is going to be speaking this Sunday on television, and he

9   wanted to make sure that everybody was there.

10   MARY: *(Very excitedly)* Really? At *(Insert church's name)*?

11   MARK: Yes! I'm excited too. Did you read the latest edition of

12   *Church News*?

13   MARY: Uh … no. What was it …

14   MARK: Oh, my! There's my call waiting. Could you call the next

15   person on the list and let them know?

16   MARY: Oh, sure! We'll talk to you later!

17   MARK: Bye now! *(MARK turns around.)*

18   MARY: *(Hangs up.)* Wow, I can't believe it! *(Insert pastor's name)* is

19   going to be on TV! No wonder he wants everyone to know!

20   *(Looks up next number on list and dials. SUSAN faces front.)*

21   SUSAN: Hello?

22   MARY: Hello, Susan? This is Mary.

23   SUSAN: Hi, Mary.

24   MARY: Listen. You aren't going to believe this, but the reason I'm

25   calling is because next Sunday's sermon is going to be broad-

26   cast live on TV from *(Insert church's name)*.

27   SUSAN: What?!

28   MARY: I know! I couldn't believe it either! It'll be broadcast —

29   probably on channel five — all over the city! We'll be just like

30   *(Insert local church's name that has a Sunday worship broadcast)*!

31   SUSAN: Wow! How did he manage to pull that off?

32   MARY: I don't know! But I guess he had an article in *Church News*

33   this month. Anyway *(Insert pastor's name)* wants to make sure

34   that everybody knows, so could you call whoever's next on the

35   phone tree? It looks like *(Looks at list)* Lois. Could you let

1 her know?

2 SUSAN: You bet! I'll talk to you later!

3 MARY: OK! Bye! *(They hang up. MARY turns around and SUSAN*

4 *immediately dials LOIS, who faces front.)*

5 LOIS: Hello?

6 SUSAN: Hi, Lois. This is Susan. You're not going to believe this, but

7 channel five is going to be at *(Insert church's name)* next week

8 to broadcast *(Insert pastor's name)*'s sermon!

9 LOIS: You're kidding!

10 SUSAN: No! I guess that *(Insert other denomination name)* guy won't

11 be the only one on the air. They're going to give the *(Insert*

12 *your denomination's name)* some air time, too!

13 LOIS: Wow! And what great timing! *(Insert pastor's name)* is really

14 excited about next Sunday's message on two-way communi-

15 cation within the church.

16 SUSAN: Oh, yeah? Is that the same one that he wrote up in the

17 latest edition of *Church News*?

18 LOIS: I didn't know he had an article in *Church News*!

19 SUSAN: Oh, yeah! It's terrific! Well, listen, I've got to go shopping

20 for a new outfit for Sunday. What on earth do you wear to be

21 on TV?

22 LOIS: I have no idea! I guess I'll see you Sunday! Thanks for the

23 news!

24 SUSAN: Sure thing. That's what phone trees are for! *(Hangs up.)*

25 LOIS: *(Pauses, looking a bit confused.)* Hey, I thought *I* usually

26 started the phone tree!

27

28

29

30

31

32

33

34

35

The Prophet Margin

*A sketch looking at those who claim to be
something they are not.*

Theme: False prophets

**Scripture
Reference:**   Matthew 7:15-23

Synopsis: The only thing a "telephony" psychic can
predict is what her customers want to hear.

Cast: Supervisor
Psychic
Customer

Props: Two telephones.

Setting: Stage Right is the "Psychic Companions Hotline" telemarketing talk room. Stage Left is the
customer's house. Place a telephone and a
table and chair at each location.

1   *(PSYCHIC and SUPERVISOR are at Stage Right. PSYCHIC sits*
2   *and SUPERVISOR stands. CUSTOMER sits at Stage Left, dialing*
3   *his telephone.)*
4   **SUPERVISOR: Remember, keep your answers generic and hope-**
5   **ful! Tell people they're going to have good relationships and**
6   **make a lot more money in the future. And remember, they're**
7   **paying with a credit card, so chances are they're all in debt —**
8   **use that info if it helps.** *(SUPERVISOR exits.)*
9   **PSYCHIC:** *(Picking up telephone)* **Psychic Companions Hotline! To**
10   **whom am I speaking?**
11   **CUSTOMER: What?**
12   **PSYCHIC: Hello? Who is making a psychic connection?**
13   **CUSTOMER: You mean you don't know?**
14   **PSYCHIC: What?**
15   **CUSTOMER: Are you a psychic?**
16   **PSYCHIC: Yes, sir** *(or ma'am)* **I am — this is the Psychic Compan-**
17   **ions Hotline!**
18   **CUSTOMER: Then why should I have to tell you who I am? You**
19   **should already know that.**
20   **PSYCHIC:** *(Chuckling)* **Yes, well, uh … the psychic connection is**
21   **much stronger in person than over the phone. So, your name?**
22   **CUSTOMER: Oh. Ben.**
23   **PSYCHIC: OK, Ben, what's your birthdate?**
24   **CUSTOMER: August 28, 1973. But shouldn't you already**
25   **know that?**
26   **PSYCHIC: I … uh … I did. We always ask that to verify that you**
27   **are the person we think you are.**
28   **CUSTOMER: Huh?**
29   **PSYCHIC: Now Ben, what things would you like to know?**
30   **CUSTOMER: Well, I'm not very happy with my job — listen, are**
31   **you for real?**
32   **PSYCHIC: Of course I am, Ben. But then you** *would* **ask me that —**
33   **you're very skeptical by nature.**
34   **CUSTOMER: Wow! I** *am* **very skeptical! How'd you know that?**
35   **PSYCHIC: I'm a psychic, Ben. Now let's talk about your future. I**

1   definitely see a change in your personal life. You've been
2   dating around, but not very successfully, right?
3 CUSTOMER: Wow! Yeah, I have!
4 PSYCHIC: Well, I see a change in that. You're going to meet some-
5   one and fall in love. After a while the relationship will
6   intensify, at which time it could go one of two ways, but that's
7   still up in the air.
8 CUSTOMER: Wow!
9 PSYCHIC: As for your future, I definitely see you having a change
10   in your career.
11 CUSTOMER: Really?
12 PSYCHIC: Your boss will give you reason to wish to go elsewhere.
13 CUSTOMER: Wow. She already has.
14 PSYCHIC: The new job you seek should be something completely
15   different than what you've been doing. The field you're in is
16   definitely wrong for you.
17 CUSTOMER: I've always felt that!
18 PSYCHIC: Your new job will pay much more than your current
19   one. I see lots more spendable cash in your future. You'll be
20   able to pay down that credit card balance of yours in no time.
21 CUSTOMER: Wow! How did you know about that?
22 PSYCHIC: We've been through this. Anything else?
23 CUSTOMER: Oh, yeah. Well, I've been thinking a lot about my
24   soul lately.
25 PSYCHIC: Your soul?
26 CUSTOMER: Yeah. You know — eternity.
27 PSYCHIC: Well, I believe that we all have souls that live forever.
28   Live it the best way you can and your station will improve
29   after this earthly life is done.
30 CUSTOMER: *(Pause)* That's it?
31 PSYCHIC: Pretty much.
32 CUSTOMER: What about church and God and all that stuff?
33 PSYCHIC: Do what you feel comfortable with to get you by. It's
34   your inner peace that will get you through.
35 CUSTOMER: OK. Gee, thanks!

1   PSYCHIC: Thank you for calling the Psychic Companions
2   Hotline!
3   SUPERVISOR *(Walks up and puts his/her hand on Psychic's shoul-*
4   *der.)* Listen, I've been going over the weekly reports and your
5   minutes-per-call average is way down. I'm afraid you're not
6   really cut out for this kind of work. I'm sorry.
7   PSYCHIC: *(Sitting there stunned for a moment.)* Really? Huh. Never
8   saw that coming! *(All exit.)*
9
10
11
12
13
14
15
16
17
18
19
20
21
22
23
24
25
26
27
28
29
30
31
32
33
34
35

Puppy in a Box

*A sketch about how we look at and value life
in the modern scientific world.*

Theme: Sanctity of life

**Scripture
References:** Colossians 1:16, Psalms 139:13-14

Synopsis: Wacky scientist Mr. Wizard is back, and this
time he sets about making a puppy — again,
with dubious results.

Cast: Mr. Wizard
Hope

Props: Any type of box. A hinged lid is nice but not
necessary.

**Sound
Effects:** Loud growl (using Off-stage microphone).

Setting: Mr. Wizard's lab. The box sits at Center Stage.

1   HOPE: Whatcha doin', Mr. Wizard?

2   MR. WIZARD: Oh, hey, Hope! Oh, this? I'm making a puppy!

3   HOPE: You're *what?*

4   MR. WIZARD: I'm making a puppy.

5   HOPE: You can't make a puppy in a box!

6   MR. WIZARD: Oh, you'd be surprised, little girl. This is the

7   nineties, *(or "new millennium")* after all ...

8   HOPE: Really?

9   MR. WIZARD: Oh, yeah! We can make anything — a puppy, a

10   flower ... even another you.

11   HOPE: I don't think so. *Nobody* could make another me. Except

12   maybe my parents ...

13   MR. WIZARD: Oh, yeah? Modern science can make anything God

14   can make. Maybe better. Want to help?

15   HOPE: I don't think so. You can't mean that *you're* as good as God.

16   MR. WIZARD: Oh, yeah! Anything at all. What's your favorite

17   kind of dog?

18   HOPE: Uh, a little terrier, I guess. You know, I would be awfully

19   careful if I were you.

20   MR. WIZARD: Oh, yeah? How's that?

21   HOPE: Well there's more to making a puppy than molecules

22   and cells.

23   MR. WIZARD: Not really. Male or female?

24   HOPE: Uh, female, I guess. Where does God fit into this whole

25   picture?

26   MR. WIZARD: God? Who needs God? This is the age of informa-

27   tion. We are God. Uh, what's your favorite color?

28   HOPE: Mmmm ... purple. *(MR. WIZARD pauses, shrugs his shoulders,*

29   *and dumps something in the box.)* Aren't you afraid something

30   might go wrong?

31   MR. WIZARD: Like?

32   HOPE: Like ... I dunno. Lots of things. Like it doesn't turn out

33   perfect?

34   MR. WIZARD: Easy. We start over.

35   HOPE: What happens if you finish and nobody wants it?

1   MR. WIZARD: Hmmm. I guess we'd just destroy it and make
2   another one when they did want it. Curly hair or straight?
3   HOPE: Straight. But what about the sanctity of life? Life isn't just
4   chemistry.
5   MR. WIZARD: Sanctity of life?
6   HOPE: Yeah. Life is too precious to mess around with.
7   MR. WIZARD: Where do you get this stuff?
8   HOPE: The Bible! It says in Psalms that God knows us before we are
9   even born. And that we are fearfully and wonderfully made.
10 MR. WIZARD: *(Pause)* Well, this is cool ...
11 HOPE: Don't you see? If you get too used to making life and
12   destroying life, it won't mean very much anymore.
13 MR. WIZARD: Oh, sure it does. What color eyes?
14 HOPE: Oh, no. I don't want anything to do with this. I like puppies
15   the old-fashioned way. *(HOPE walks off.)*
16 MR. WIZARD: Wait! Your puppy's done! *(Pause)* Oh well, I could
17   use a dog. *(Opens box and a huge growl is heard. MR. WIZARD*
18   *gasps.)* Uh, Hope? What was that Scripture again?
19
20
21
22
23
24
25
26
27
28
29
30
31
32
33
34
35

Really...Don't Mention It!

A sketch emphasizing what a difference a kind word makes.

Theme: Encouragement

Scripture Reference: 2 Corinthians 7:5-16

Synopsis: A weary waitperson is on the verge of quitting when a well-timed compliment lifts her spirits.

Cast: Shelly
Kara
Manager

Props: A stack of bills (real or play money), purse.

Setting: A restaurant. There are no customers, as it is at the end of a shift.

1   (*KARA is counting her money and looking very discouraged.*
2   *SHELLY approaches.*)
3   SHELLY: Hey, Kara. You do any good tonight?
4   KARA: Not really, Shelly. I mean, the money's OK, I guess. I'm not
5   getting rich, but I'm getting by.
6   SHELLY: Then what's wrong?
7   KARA: Oh, I don't know. I think I'm gonna quit.
8   SHELLY: What? You've been a waitress here for as long as I can
9   remember!
10 KARA: I know.
11 SHELLY: I mean, you were here forever when I was hired three
12   years ago.
13 KARA: Yeah, I remember.
14 SHELLY: I remember the boss saying how you had been the senior
15   waitperson since he was hired.
16 KARA: (*Getting irritated*) Uh-huh. What are you getting at?
17 SHELLY: Just that you've been here since ...
18 KARA: Look, is this supposed to be helping?
19 SHELLY: Sorry! Why are you thinking about quitting?
20 KARA: Oh, I don't know. I just feel beaten down.
21 SHELLY: Who doesn't?
22 KARA: Yeah, I know. But don't you ever get tired of of it all?
23 SHELLY: What do you mean?
24 KARA: I mean, what do you remember about tonight?
25 SHELLY: Tonight? (*Pause*) Well, I guess bringing out the wrong
26   order to table six was a highlight. Or getting that fifty cent tip
27   on that twenty dollar check.
28 KARA: That's what I'm talking about.
29 SHELLY: What?
30 KARA: I mean, it's so negative. I dropped a club sandwich on the
31   floor to start the night. I messed up the orders on three
32   different tables. I poured water into a man's lap on table nine.
33 SHELLY: So that's what that scream was!
34 KARA: I got iced tea in my shoe at seven o'clock and I still squish
35   when I walk. And I overheard two ladies talking about my

1   varicose veins. And for what? Thirty-nine dollars and fifty
2   cents. My back hurts. And I saw a couple of customers talking
3   to Jeff — I know he's going to talk to me about their complaint.
4   SHELLY: I guess I see what you mean.
5   KARA: Everyone's got something to complain about. I'm just tired
6   of it.
7   SHELLY: Oh Kara. That's the way it is in every job. You never hear
8   about the good stuff. Remember what you heard most as a
9   kid? Stop that! Get down! Let go! Get your sister out of the
10   dryer! All negative.
11   KARA: I suppose you're right. But it's worse in this business. I'm
12   getting out.
13   SHELLY: Why don't you go home and get some sleep? I'm sure
14   you'll feel better about things tomorrow night.
15   KARA: I'm telling you, I don't think I'll be here. I'm scanning the
16   classifieds tomorrow. *(Enter MANAGER.)*
17   MANAGER: Kara, you got a minute?
18   KARA: *(Under her breath)* Here we go. *(To MANAGER)* Yeah, Jeff?
19   MANAGER: You were the waitress on table thirteen tonight, right?
20   KARA: Yeah?
21   Manager: Well, they made a special point to talk to me as they were
22   leaving.
23   KARA: Listen, Jeff ….
24   MANAGER: Let me finish. They said that they go out to eat all the
25   time, all over the world, and in the twenty-five years they've
26   been dining out …
27   KARA: Oh brother …
28   MANAGER: They've never had a dining experience as good as the
29   one they had tonight.
30   KARA: What?
31   MANAGER: Nice job, Kara. They said they're writing a letter to
32   the main office. You make us all look good. *(Pats her on the*
33   *shoulder as he leaves.)*
34   KARA: *(To herself)* How do you like that?
35   SHELLY: *(Pauses as she messes with her purse on the way out. Smiles*

1   *at KARA as she leaves.)* **See ya tomorrow, Kara.** *(Pauses again*
2   *before leaving.)*
3   **KARA:** *(As both are leaving)* **Yeah. See ya tomorrow, Shelly.**
4
5
6
7
8
9
10
11
12
13
14
15
16
17
18
19
20
21
22
23
24
25
26
27
28
29
30
31
32
33
34
35

A Tangled Web

A sketch on being honest.

Theme: Lying, dishonesty

Scripture Reference: Proverbs 12:22

Synopsis: A guy who feels his life isn't exciting enough stretches the truth to impress an old crush — then discovers she's living a life that's every bit as ordinary as his.

Cast: Bob
Sandie
Extras (party-goers)

Props: Two cups, name tags for everyone.

Sound Effects: Bob's audible thoughts (preferably on tape, but may be spoken Off-stage by someone other than Bob), Off-stage voice (spoken into microphone Off-stage).

Setting: A high school reunion.

1 *(Enter BOB, with a cup of punch in his hand. SANDIE is standing*
2 *Stage Left with a cup in her hand as well, talking to another of the*
3 *party-goers. BOB waits until a lull in the conversation before*
4 *interrupting. The person she was talking to says good-bye at the*
5 *end of the thought monolog. Before he approaches her, however,*
6 *his thoughts are heard [on tape, preferably, but may be spoken*
7 *into a microphone by someone Off-stage].)*
8 BOB'S VOICE: Oh, brother. I hate class reunions! Just another
9 opportunity to remind myself of what a loser I am! A high
10 school English teacher who writes screenplays that will never
11 be published. Oh, that's attractive. No wonder you never
12 married, Bob. *(Pause)* Well, not tonight! Tonight I'm going to
13 be successful! I look good, I've got the rented BMW, and for
14 one night, I'm not going to be a high school English teacher
15 with no prospect for real success. Now all I need to do is find
16 someone to talk to. *(Looking around)* Oh, my goodness! Is that
17 her? Sandie? Oh, this is perfect! I'll just wait until she's done
18 talking to that loser, and then ... *(The other person walks Off-*
19 *stage, saying good-bye. SANDIE is looking the other way as he*
20 *approaches and very obviously looks at her name tag.)*
21 BOB: Sandie? Sandie Miller? Is that you?
22 SANDIE: Yes. And you are ... *(Looking at his name tag)* Bob
23 Frederick?
24 BOB: Yeah! Well, I used to go by Bobby, but ...
25 SANDIE: Bobby? Oh, my goodness! Bobby Freddy! How long has
26 it been?
27 BOB: *(Chuckling at the obviousness of her question)* Well ...
28 BOB and SANDIE: *(Together)* Twenty years!
29 SANDIE: Right! Oh my goodness, you've changed! I mean, you
30 look great!
31 BOB: You too! I mean the looking great part! You haven't changed
32 one bit.
33 SANDIE: Aw, that's sweet of you! So, what have you been doing
34 with your life?
35 BOB: Well ... *(Pausing, obviously trying to come up with something to*

1   *impress her.)* **After medical school, I went on to practice at the**

2   **Mayo clinic ...**

3 **SANDIE: Wow! Really?**

4 **BOB: Uh, yeah! It's kinda boring, but it's a living!**

5 **SANDIE: So what's your specialty?**

6 **BOB: Pardon?**

7 **SANDIE: You're a doctor. What's your specialty?**

8 **BOB: Oh! Right. My specialty is ...** *(Pauses briefly)* **Cardio ...**

9   **pulmonary ... angioplastics ... But it's too boring to talk**

10   **about ...**

11 **SANDIE: Oh, nonsense! So you live out in Minnesota?**

12 **BOB: Huh?**

13 **SANDIE: Where the Mayo clinic is, I mean.**

14 **BOB: Oh, yes. Minnesota! No. No, I don't. Not all the time, I mean.**

15 **SANDIE: You commute?**

16 **BOB: Well, ... sort of. I spend my months off around here, and then**

17   **jet back to ... Minnesota when they need me to be there.**

18 **SANDIE: Wow! Sounds exciting!**

19 **BOB: Oh, you know! It doesn't leave much time for enjoying the**

20   **finer things in life — like my BMW and such. I mean,**

21   **tonight's practically the only night I've gotten to take it out in**

22   **... I don't know when!**

23 **SANDIE: My! You've done quite well for yourself.**

24 **BOB: Well, you know. There's a price. Still single, for example. No**

25   **time to meet people ...**

26 **SANDIE: Oh?**

27 **BOB: Yeah!** *(Pause)* **Between that and running my own practice on**

28   **the coast ...**

29 **SANDIE: Wow! The coast?**

30 **BOB: Yeah. You know ... that west coast ... thing ...**

31 **SANDIE: How do you find the time?**

32 **BOB: Oh, you manage.** *(Pause)* **So, enough about me. What have**

33   **you been up to?**

34 **SANDIE: Me? Oh, nothing really ...**

35 **BOB: Oh, come on! Head cheerleader, class president, smartest girl**

1   in the class — what did you end up doing?

2   SANDIE: Oh, I became an English teacher. Got married. Had two

3   kids. Got divorced. you know the drill.

4   BOB: Really? *(Pause)* Oh, I'm sorry.

5   SANDIE: For what? The kids are great. The youngest one just went

6   off to college this fall ...

7   BOB: Wow. Time flies.

8   SANDIE: So you're a doctor, huh?

9   BOB: Yeah. Tell me more about your teaching ...

10   SANDIE: Oh, I'm not teaching anymore.

11   BOB: Oh?

12   SANDIE: No. After the divorce, I decided that I loved writing so

13   much that I'd try to do something with it.

14   BOB: Really? What happened?

15   SANDIE: Sold a few plays and a book. Nothing much, really. But

16   enough to let me do what I really wanted to do.

17   BOB: Which is?

18   SANDIE: Open my own agency. I find writers who haven't found

19   their market yet and try to help them get their start.

20   BOB: *(Getting the idea that he should've been honest, he looks crest-*

21   *fallen.)* You don't say?

22   SANDIE: I remember how hard it was to get my foot in the door.

23   It's really quite rewarding to be able to help out those who

24   might be struggling ...

25   BOB: *(Pause)* I'll bet.

26   SANDIE: Well, anyway ... it was great to see you again, Bobby!

27   BOB: *(In shock)* Yeah. Great.

28   SANDIE: I'm glad to see you so happy and successful. Some of us

29   have it and some of us don't, I guess.

30   BOB: I guess.

31   SANDIE: Well, I'll let you catch up with some of the old gang.

32   *(Looks at her watch.)* I'm supposed to meet Nori Yost here

33   tonight — remember her? She's a writer, and I think I'm

34   going to produce one of her plays. Isn't that exciting?

35   BOB: Nori? Oh, yeah. Nori. Exciting.

1   SANDIE: It was good seeing you again, Bobby. You take care, OK?

2   BOB: Yeah! It was good to see you again too, Sandie. Good luck

3   with that play. And tell Nori I said hi.

4   SANDIE: Sure will. See ya! *(Exits.)*

5   BOB: Yeah, see ya, Sandie. *(Long pause while he contemplates what*

6   *he has done.)*

7   OFF-STAGE VOICE: Would the owner of a blue BMW please

8   come to the reception area? There's been a minor accident ...

9   BOB: Oh, no! I didn't take out the rental insurance! *(Exits quickly.)*

10

11

12

13

14

15

16

17

18

19

20

21

22

23

24

25

26

27

28

29

30

31

32

33

34

35

Thanks a Lot!

A sketch on giving thanks in all circumstances.

Theme:	Thanksgiving
Scripture Reference:	1 Thessalonians 5:18
Synopsis:	Two people who have been stranded on a desert island hold sharply contrasting views of their situation.
Cast:	Ivan Sherman
Props:	None.
Setting:	The beach of a desert island.

1	(*IVAN and SHERMAN are on a beach. IVAN is whistling and*
2	*carefree. SHERMAN is tense and uptight. He mocks IVAN, blam-*
3	*ing his attitude on ignorance.*)
4	**IVAN:** (*Stretching and smiling*) **Ah! What a gorgeous day! Don't you**
5	**think so, Sherman?**
6	**SHERMAN:** (*Sarcastically*) **Oh, yeah. We're having some fun now!**
7	**IVAN: Ah, come on! It's beautiful! You can see for miles and**
8	**miles!**
9	**SHERMAN: Uh, hello?** (*Knocking on his head, then yelling*) **We're**
10	**on a desert island, you moron! You can always see for miles!**
11	**IVAN: Well, yeah! That's one of the great things about living on**
12	**this island! Can't you see that?**
13	**SHERMAN: Look. If our boat hadn't sunk last month, neither of**
14	**us would even be here! So don't pretend you're happy about**
15	**something that we obviously didn't plan for.**
16	**IVAN: Why not? After all, we both should've drowned. You know,**
17	**you should be thankful!**
18	**SHERMAN: I'm jumpin' for joy, all right. It's just another day at**
19	**the beach …**
20	**IVAN: Look. I know we didn't plan for it, but can't you see that**
21	**there are certainly things to be thankful for?**
22	**SHERMAN: Like what? Being alive?!**
23	**IVAN: For starters, yes. And for being stranded with such a won-**
24	**derfully uplifting conversational partner, eh?**
25	**SHERMAN: Oh, yeah. I forgot. Man! It's like being stranded with**
26	**a stinking cheerleading squad!**
27	**IVAN: And it's a tropical climate! By the way, have I mentioned**
28	**what a great tan you're getting?**
29	**SHERMAN: Yeah? Thanks! You know, I've been working on it.**
30	(*Pause*) **EVERY SINGLE DAY! THERE'S NOTHING ELSE**
31	**TO DO! Now, leave me alone!**
32	**IVAN:** (*Pause*) **You know, I'm really not sure I like your attitude …**
33	**SHERMAN: So move out!**
34	**IVAN: Ha-ha. I'm only saying that you have a lot of reasons to be**
35	**thankful, yet you only seem to find the negative side of things.**

1   SHERMAN: *(Slowly)* **Let me put this simply.** *(Pause)* **We are stranded**
2   **on a desert island. Alone. With very little hope of rescue. There**
3   **are hundreds more negative things than positive things in our**
4   **lives right now.**
5   IVAN: **Nope.**
6   SHERMAN: **Excuse me?**
7   IVAN: **I said nope. For every negative thing, I'm sure there is a**
8   **positive side.**
9   SHERMAN: **Oh, really?**
10   IVAN: **Yep. Come on. Try me.**
11   SHERMAN: **All right, I will.** *(Pause)* **We are stranded, miles away**
12   **from civilization.**
13   IVAN: **We have been given the opportunity to escape the rat race**
14   **for a while.**
15   SHERMAN: **All right, all right.** *(Pause)* **We have just the clothes on**
16   **our backs — no wardrobe.**
17   IVAN: **We are minimalists. Simplicity is our motto.**
18   SHERMAN: **We eat fish, pineapple, and coconut every day.**
19   IVAN: **Tropical menu!**
20   SHERMAN: *(Getting increasingly angry)* **We live in a hut!**
21   IVAN: **No taxes!**
22   SHERMAN: **Snakes and bugs!**
23   IVAN: **Wildlife!**
24   SHERMAN: *(More angry)* **Exposure!**
25   IVAN: **Healthy glow!**
26   SHERMAN: *(Pause)* **OK, how about this? The only other person on**
27   **the island you are on is *going to kill you!* *(He lunges for IVAN***
28   *and starts to choke him.)*
29   IVAN: *(Struggling to talk through the strangling process)* **Recreational**
30   **... Opp ... or ... tun ... i ... ties ...** *(SHERMAN loosens his hold,*
31   *seeing it is no use.)*
32   SHERMAN: **AAAAHHH!** *(Letting go, rising, and walking around)*
33   **It's no use! I give up.**
34   IVAN: *(Rising to a sitting position and wiping himself off)* **I knew**
35   **you would.**

1   SHERMAN: Whatever! *(Pause)* You know, I don't understand how
2   you do that!
3   IVAN: Do what?
4   SHERMAN: How you stay upbeat all the time.
5   IVAN: It's easy! You just look for things to be thankful for in every
6   situation.
7   SHERMAN: But that's impossible sometimes!
8   IVAN: Not impossible. It's harder sometimes, but it's always possible.
9   SHERMAN: Really? *(Pause)* I guess I see your point.
10   IVAN: Of course you do. There are hundreds of opportunities to try
11   it out every single day.
12   SHERMAN: I guess so ...
13   IVAN: Take that ship, for example.
14   SHERMAN: What ship?
15   IVAN: That one over there that just passed the island. *(IVAN points*
16   *off onto the horizon.)* If we had started waving our arms and
17   jumping up and down when I first saw it five minutes ago,
18   they might have seen us.
19   SHERMAN: *(Pause as SHERMAN stares at IVAN incredulously.)*
20   What?! You saw that ship five minutes ago and you're just
21   now telling me?
22   IVAN: Yeah. Anyway, if we had ...
23   SHERMAN: But if we would've gotten their attention, we might
24   have been rescued!
25   IVAN: Right. That's what I'm saying. If we would've gotten their
26   attention, we might have been rescued, and we never
27   would've had this great bonding time! *(IVAN puts his arm*
28   *around SHERMAN's shoulder.)* Old buddy!
29   SHERMAN: *(Pauses as he looks like he's going to cry. He points out*
30   *toward the ship.)* We could have been rescued ...
31   IVAN: And another thing to be thankful for?
32   SHERMAN: *(Still in shock)* What's that?
33   IVAN: I don't think that ship was very nice. I didn't see any pool
34   deck or any fancy umbrellas. It was probably one of those
35   budget cruises or something ...

1 **SHERMAN: So?!**

2 **IVAN: Well, I'm just saying that the next boat that comes by will be**

3   **much nicer. Don't you think? That's lucky!**

4 **SHERMAN: But ... but ... but ...** *(He stares out toward the ship,*

5   *mumbling and pointing.)*

6 **IVAN: Well, I'm off to get lunch for us. Does fish sound OK?**

7   *(Pause)* **Sherman?**

8 **SHERMAN: But ... but ... but ...** *(Still pointing and staring)*

9 **IVAN:** *(Pats him on the shoulder.)* **Hang in there, buddy! I'll be back**

10   **in a flash!** *(He exits.)*

11 **SHERMAN: But ... but ... but ...** *(Throws up his hands in frustra-*

12   *tion.)* **Ohhhhh ...** *(Exits, still mumbling.)*

13

14

15

16

17

18

19

20

21

22

23

24

25

26

27

28

29

30

31

32

33

34

35

These Are the Good Old Days

A sketch looking at preoccupation with the way things were instead of focusing on what's ahead.

Theme: Looking toward the future

Scripture Reference: Isaiah 42:9

Synopsis: A father dismisses his children's computer games, believing that his generation was the last of the truly hard workers. But he is brought up short by the reality that things were not nearly as austere as he remembers.

Cast: Child 1
Child 2
Dad
Grandparent

Props: Newspaper.

Setting: A family living room. The kids are home from school on a snow day. Place three chairs at Center Stage.

1   *(Two CHILDREN are sitting and looking bored while DAD sits*
2   *reading a paper.)*
3   **CHILD 1:** Man, this is boring! There's nothing to do.
4   **CHILD 2:** No kidding! A snow day is usually something I live for.
5   But this is too much! It even knocked out the cable!
6   **CHILD 1:** I guess we could watch another video. *(They look at each*
7   *other.)*
8   **TOGETHER:** Nah! *(DAD snickers to himself.)*
9   **DAD:** Oh, brother!
10   **CHILD 1:** What?
11   **DAD:** Oh, it's just sad, that's all.
12   **CHILD 2:** What's sad?
13   **DAD:** It's sad that two young, creative people can't come up with
14   something to entertain themselves when they have some
15   unexpected free time.
16   **CHILD 1:** Well, give us some ideas, then.
17   **DAD:** See, that's the trouble with you kids today. You always want
18   somebody else to do the work instead of figuring it out for
19   yourselves. It wasn't like that when I was a kid.
20   **CHILD 2:** Well, what did you do when you had a snow day?
21   **DAD:** First of all, we never had snow days. If it snowed three feet
22   like it did here last night, we were expected to be at school
23   early to help shovel the sidewalks clear.
24   **CHILD 1:** Oh, brother. Here we go …
25   **DAD:** And we walked to school, regardless of how bad it was. With-
26   out complaining about it.
27   **CHILD 2:** In three feet of snow.
28   **DAD:** Or more! But when we did have free time, we didn't waste it
29   on TV and video games.
30   **CHILD 1:** Because you didn't have TV, right?
31   **DAD:** Oh, yeah. We had TV. Three channels. On a clear day.
32   **CHILD 2:** Wow. That'd be rough.
33   **DAD:** Nah. It was better then. We had to come up with our own fun.
34   **CHILD 1:** I think it's better now. You want to play a computer game
35   with me?

1   DAD: See? That's what I'm talking about. We didn't have
2   computers. We had to figure things out for ourselves. Use our
3   minds!
4   CHILD 2: But Dad, most of the computer games we have are really
5   challenging — they make you figure out puzzles and mind-
6   teasers and really make you think!
7   DAD: In my day, you didn't need a computer to help you think. You
8   thought because you had to! Like deciding what to do on a
9   snow day.
10   CHILD 1: Like what?
11   DAD: See?
12   CHILD 2: No, really, what did you do with your spare time?
13   DAD: *(Pausing and fumbling for words)* Well, uh … well — we didn't
14   have any free time! We all had jobs.
15   CHILD 1: Oh, brother. We've been here before …
16   DAD: Forty hours a week. And chores on top of it.
17   CHILD 2: But Dad, surely there were times when you didn't know
18   what to do.
19   DAD: If that ever happened, we'd invent things. Why, one day
20   when your uncle was sick in bed with a fever of a hundred and
21   eight degrees, he invented the Ziploc bag.
22   CHILD 1: He did not.
23   DAD: Did too.
24   CHILD 2: Dad, the Ziploc bag was invented in 1964 by Howard
25   Lipstock.
26   DAD: What?
27   CHILD 1: It was one of many inventions he came up with while
28   trying to invent something else. I just read that on the com-
29   puter encyclopedia.
30   DAD: Really. Well, did it say on that encyclopedia of yours that he
31   stole the idea from your Uncle Hank?
32   CHILD 2: Didn't notice it.
33   DAD: Anyway, that's not the point. The point is, we were more cre-
34   ative then. *(Enter GRANDPARENT.)* Why, I remember one
35   time, Hank and I were playing with Lincoln Logs and …

1 GRANDPARENT: Kids, the cookies you guys made this morning
2   are done!
3 CHILD 1: Thanks, Grandma! Come on, Joel, let's have some while
4   we play a game of Myst.
5 CHILD 2: *(Exiting with CHILD 1)* Yeah!
6 GRANDPARENT: Well, I sure wish the computer had been around
7   when you and your brother had snow days.
8 DAD: What are you talking about?
9 GRANDPARENT: Well, it just seems like kids are getting more and
10   more creative — they seem more industrious. Gives me a lot
11   of hope for the future.
12 DAD: Are you serious? We used to make our own fun!
13 GRANDPARENT: Ha! When you guys had snow days, you sat
14   around the house and fought with each other over whether to
15   watch *Captain Kangaroo* or *Bugs Bunny*.
16 DAD: What?
17 GRANDPARENT: *(Laughing)* Then there was that one time your
18   idiot brother Hank wrapped the cat up in Saran Wrap. Some-
19   times I wondered about you two.
20 DAD: I just remember working a lot more when I was a kid ...
21 GRANDPARENT: You had a paper route. And I used to have to remind
22   you every day. If I had a dime for every paper I folded ...
23 DAD: All right, all right.
24 GRANDPARENT: Yep, kids today are getting more and more
25   creative. But it's still not like when I was a kid. *(Rising to her feet*
26   *and starting to exit)* We were really the creative generation...
27 DAD: Oh, brother, here we go ...
28 GRANDPARENT: *(Exiting with DAD)* Did I ever tell you about the
29   blizzard of '48, when your Aunt Sarah invented Teflon?
30
31
32
33
34
35

Two Roads Diverged...

A sketch about choosing the right path.

Theme: Making decisions

Scripture Reference: Jeremiah 6:16

Synopsis: A hiker is paralyzed with indecision when confronted with a fork in the road. The reason? She doesn't know her final destination.

Cast: Hiker 1
Hiker 2

Props: None.

Setting: A woodland path.

1   *(HIKER 1 sits with head resting in hands, elbows on knees.*

2   *HIKER 2 enters.)*

3   **HIKER 2:** *(Passing by)* **Hey. How's it going?**

4   **HIKER 1: Hi.**

5   **HIKER 2:** *(Already past HIKER 1, but sensing something is wrong,*

6   *turns back toward him. After a pause ...)* **Is everything all right?**

7   **HIKER 1: What do you mean?**

8   **HIKER 2: Well, I mean ... are you hurt? Or just resting?**

9   **HIKER 1: Neither, really.**

10   **HIKER 2:** *(Pause, confused)* **I mean, it's just not that common to see**

11   **someone on the trail that's just ... stopped. You know?**

12   **HIKER 1: Yeah, I suppose you're right.**

13   **HIKER 2: So, you need help or anything?**

14   **HIKER 1: Well, yeah ... I guess.**

15   **HIKER 2:** *(Pause)* **What seems to be the trouble?**

16   **HIKER 1: Well, see ... I was just walking along, see. And I'm**

17   **making pretty good time and all, but then I came upon this**

18   **fork in the road.**

19   **HIKER 2: Yeah?**

20   **HIKER 1:** *(Pause)* **Well, that's it.**

21   **HIKER 2: What's it?**

22   **HIKER 1: This fork in the road. I don't know which path to take.**

23   **HIKER 2: Oh! I see. Well, I might be able to help. Where are you going?**

24   **HIKER 1: Well, I guess I won't know until I decide which path I'm on.**

25   **HIKER 2: No. I mean, where is it that you WANT to go?**

26   **HIKER 1: Well, that's just it. I'm not really sure.**

27   **HIKER 2: I see.** *(Pause)* **So you started out this way and didn't really**

28   **know where you'd end up?**

29   **HIKER 1: Basically. I mean, I know I want to go in this general**

30   **direction,** *(Motioning)* **but as you can see, these paths are both**

31   **going that way. So I'm not sure which one to take.**

32   **HIKER 2: Uh-huh. Well, how important is it that you end up in a**

33   **specific place?**

34   **HIKER 1: Very important. It's the most important thing to me.**

35   **HIKER 2: But you don't know where that is?**

1 HIKER 1: Not a clue.
2 HIKER 2: So how are you going to decide?
3 HIKER 1: This is my problem.
4 HIKER 2: I see. So how are you going to solve this problem?
5 HIKER 1: I have no idea.
6 HIKER 2: And how long have you been sitting there?
7 HIKER 1: Well, *(Pause)* what's today?
8 HIKER 2: You mean you've been out here overnight?
9 HIKER 1: No! *(Pause)* Been at least three nights. Is this Thursday?
10 HIKER 2: Look. This is silly. You've got to make a decision. You'll
11   starve to death out here. Or freeze. Or something.
12 HIKER 1: I am kinda hungry.
13 HIKER 2: Listen, in all that time, didn't anybody else come by?
14 HIKER 1: Oh, yeah! Lots of folks.
15 HIKER 2: And which path did they choose?
16 HIKER 1: Well, see, that's just it. Some have chosen this way, and
17   some have chosen that way. It's too confusing.
18 HIKER 2: Look, you can't stay out here forever. You've got to
19   choose one or the other.
20 HIKER 1: But how?
21 HIKER 2: At this point, that shouldn't be your biggest problem.
22   You're going to die if you just sit there.
23 HIKER 1: I suppose you're right. Which way are you going? *(He rises.)*
24 HIKER 2: I'm going this way. You're welcome to tag along if
25   you'd like.
26 HIKER 1: Thanks. But how do I know the path you choose will be
27   the right one?
28 HIKER 2: Well ... *(Pause)* I guess you can't know for sure ...
29 HIKER 1: I mean, they both look like good paths, but if they were
30   both so right, there'd only be one of them, right?
31 HIKER 2: I suppose so.
32 HIKER 1: Have you ever gone down either one before?
33 HIKER 2: Well, no ...
34 HIKER 1: So you really have no idea which path to take either,
35   do you?

1   **HIKER 2:** Well, not exactly, but ...

2   **HIKER 1:** You know, the more I think about it, the more I realize

3   that if I'm going to be the one walking the path, then I'd

4   better be the one to choose. I can't listen to you or anyone else.

5   **HIKER 2:** Of course. That's what you *should* do.

6   **HIKER 1:** After all, you have just as good a chance of picking the

7   wrong path as I do. Then we'd both be lost, wouldn't we?

8   **HIKER 2:** Well, I don't know about lost ...

9   **HIKER 1:** I mean, who made you the ultimate authority on picking

10   the path? You've never even been on this road before.

11   **HIKER 2:** *(Pause)* True. I haven't.

12   **HIKER 1:** You know, I appreciate your help, but if I'm going to

13   make a mistake, I'd just as soon do it on my own.

14   **HIKER 2:** Yes, yes, of course.

15   **HIKER 1:** I'm tired of waiting around. I'm going to make a decision.

16   **HIKER 2:** Good for you!

17   **HIKER 1:** Well, thanks for the encouragement. I'm off! *(Takes off*

18   *confidently down a path.)*

19   **HIKER 2:** Good luck! *(He looks after him, and then toward the audi-*

20   *ence.)* **What an odd fellow!** *(HIKER 2 is now the indecisive one.*

21   *He shrugs his shoulders, then begins to take off down the path. He*

22   *stops abruptly, considering the other path. He turns around to*

23   *take the other path, begins up that one and stops. He goes back to*

24   *the first one, begins up that one and stops. Eventually, he takes off*

25   *his backpack, sits down, and sighs.)*

26

27

28

29

30

31

32

33

34

35

Use Your Head!

A sketch about using wisdom.

Theme: Wisdom

**Scripture
References:** 1 Samuel 25:24, James 1:5,6; 3:17

Synopsis: The unthinkable happens when Matt smashes up his dad's car. Fortunately, his level-headed sister helps him make the best of a bad situation.

Cast: Matt
Abby
Dad

Props: None.

Setting: A living room. Place a chair at Center Stage for Abby.

1   *(Teenager ABBY sits in the living room. Her brother MATT rushes*
2   *in, out of breath.)*
3   MATT: Abby! Abby! I gotta talk to you — where's Dad?
4   ABBY: Chill out, Matt! I don't know, I haven't seen him. What's
5   with you?
6   MATT: I'm in so much trouble!
7   ABBY: Why? What happened?
8   MATT: Oh, man! I'm dead!
9   ABBY: Matt! What happened?
10   MATT: OK, OK! *(Pause)* I sorta smashed up Dad's car!
11   ABBY: Oh, no. Please tell me you're talking about the station
12   wagon. *(MATT shakes his head no.)* Oh, Matt! Not the Lexus!
13   Dad was going to let me use that on Saturday!
14   MATT: Look, I'm the one in trouble here! What do I do?
15   ABBY: All right, all right. Let's just keep our heads here. *(Pause)*
16   You're gonna lose yours soon as Dad finds out anyway.
17   MATT: Very funny. What am I gonna do?
18   ABBY: All right. You remember Uncle Charles?
19   MATT: The one who lives in Pennsylvania?
20   ABBY: That's right. You can live with him.
21   MATT: ABBY! I'm serious! I need your help!
22   ABBY: Oh, all right. How bad is it?
23   MATT: Well, it looks a little better than the tree I backed into.
24   ABBY: Ouch. The big tree by the driveway?
25   MATT: Yeah. It's sort of scraped up. Like the right rear fender.
26   ABBY: All right. All right. *(Pause)* Does anyone else know about this?
27   MATT: No. It just happened.
28   ABBY: *(Pacing)* OK. The real question is this: What would Greg
29   and Marcia Brady do in this situation?
30   MATT: Abby, Dad is hardly Mike Brady. Give me something that
31   will work.
32   ABBY: You're right. OK, here's what you do. Tell Dad that you've
33   got a plan.
34   MATT: Which is?
35   ABBY: You're grounded from the car for a month.

1   MATT: This is *my* plan? Whose side are you on?
2   ABBY: I'm not finished. You get an estimate on the car and tell Dad
3   you're going to pay him ten dollars a week until it's paid off.
4   Plus, tell him you'll take care of the tree by checking with a
5   gardener to see what can be done to save it. And just for good
6   measure, tell him you'll take care of all the yard work for the
7   rest of the summer.
8   MATT: Man! Are you serious?
9   ABBY: Look, if you already have an appropriate plan of action
10   figured out, Dad will be impressed. You will have punished
11   yourself and made life easier for him. And he'll know that
12   you've learned an important lesson.
13 MATT: Yeah, I suppose so. But I don't know ...
14 ABBY: Quick! Here he comes!
15 MATT: Yikes! *(DAD enters. Before he can say a word, MATT speaks*
16   *up.)* Hey, Dad? Listen, I know how great you've been with the
17   car and all ...
18 DAD: Matt, you better not ...
19 MATT: But I had a slight mishap with the tree...
20 DAD: You wha —
21 MATT: Listen, Dad, I think you should ground me for two weeks —
22   no — a month.
23 DAD: Young man, you better be —
24 MATT: And I'm going to get an estimate on the car and have it
25   fixed. I know I won't be able to pay for the whole thing at
26   once, but I'll pay ten dollars a week for as long as it takes to
27   pay you back.
28 DAD: *(Pause)* Well, all right, that sounds like ...
29 MATT: And I'll do whatever I can to fix the tree — I'll even take
30   care of the yard for the rest of the year.
31 DAD: OK, I guess that ...
32 MATT: *(Hugs him; DAD looks really confused.)* I'm so sorry, Dad!
33   But I've really learned my lesson — I'll be much more care-
34   ful from now on.
35 DAD: Well, all right then. And you'll ...? OK. And ...? Right. OK.

1   **I'm going to go look at the car. I hope you've … .well … OK.**
2   *(Exits, still mumbling and wondering what happened.)*
3   **MATT: Wow. He didn't even yell! That's pretty great.**
4   **ABBY: Told ya.**
5   **MATT: Wow, Abby. You're pretty quick on your feet.**
6   **ABBY: Ah, I've got a couple years on you.**
7   **MATT: Wow, thanks. I owe you one.**
8   **ABBY: Not really.**
9   **MATT: Really? Why not?**
10 **ABBY: Oh … well … the lawn was one of my chores. Thanks.**
11 **MATT: Hey! You set me up!** *(They exit, arguing.)*
12
13
14
15
16
17
18
19
20
21
22
23
24
25
26
27
28
29
30
31
32
33
34
35

A Virtuous Man?

A sketch on patience.

Theme: Patience

**Scripture
References:** 1 Samuel 13:11-12, Exodus 34:6-7

Synopsis: A boss's frenetic pace and ruthless style leave his two employees frustrated — until they recognize just how patient God is with them.

Cast: Graham
Morgan
Boss

Props: Toaster, (muffin can be mimed), mug, large stack of papers, miscellaneous papers for the two employees' desks.

Setting: An office. Place two desks (card tables are fine) at Center Stage and a small table off to one side to hold the toaster and mug.

1   *(Two employees, GRAHAM and MORGAN, anxiously await the*
2   *arrival of the BOSS. When he arrives, it is apparent why they were*
3   *anxious. GRAHAM rushes in as MORGAN works at his desk.)*
4 **GRAHAM:** *(Out of breath from hustling in)* **Is he here yet?**
5 **MORGAN: No. Not yet. But he's due any minute!**
6 **GRAHAM: Boy, it's all I need to be late with a boss like him! At**
7   **least I beat him here.**
8 **MORGAN: Yeah! I think his head would probably explode or some-**
9   **thing. He has the patience of an I.R.S. agent at a televangelist's**
10   **audit!**
11 **GRAHAM: Shhh! Here he comes!** *(GRAHAM quickly sits at his desk.*
12   *BOSS enters, walking across the stage as rapidly as he talks.)*
13 **GRAHAM and MORGAN:** *(Musically, as they cower at their desks)*
14   **Good morning, Mr. Finkelheimer!**
15 **BOSS:** *(Very quickly)* **Humph! I'd better have the Mayer report on**
16   **my desk before my seat hits the chair and while you're at it**
17   **bring me a cup of hot joe and an English muffin with grape**
18   **jelly on it and** *I mean now — where is it?!* *(Slam door if you have*
19   *one — the key is not to slow down and to speak in a monotone*
20   *without stopping while crossing the stage quickly.)*
21 **MORGAN: I'll get right on that, sir!** *(Pause)* **Man, how do you**
22   **suppose he does that?**
23 **GRAHAM:** *(As he scrambles to get a muffin for the BOSS)* **Does what?**
24 **MORGAN: Talks that quickly without taking a breath or anything.**
25   **Do you suppose he's an alien?**
26 **GRAHAM: It wouldn't surprise me …**
27 **BOSS:** *(Coming out of his office long enough to throw a stack of papers,*
28   *the bigger the better, onto one of their desks. Once again, he*
29   *speaks quickly and in a monotone.)* **I heard that and believe me**
30   **your next evaluations will reflect it and while we're on the sub-**
31   **ject of reports I still haven't seen the Mayer report and** *where*
32   *in the world is my muffin?!* *(Slams the door.)*
33 **GRAHAM: It's coming, sir!** *(Pause, as MORGAN shuffles through*
34   *papers on his desk looking for the Mayer report.)* **Oh, man! That**
35   **guy is impossible to please.**

1   MORGAN: No kidding! You know, I had the Wilson report to him
2   ahead of time, and he nearly bit my head off because I missed
3   a semicolon on page four!
4   GRAHAM: *(To toaster)* Come on! If this muffin isn't done like now,
5   I'm going to be unemployed! Man, isn't it good that not every-
6   one is as impatient as he is?
7   MORGAN: I'll say. I think I'd go crazy if even one more person
8   had his personality! I'll bet he could find something wrong
9   with his own mother!
10   BOSS: *(Bursting through his door again)* I'm ready to read the Mayer
11   report and it's not on my desk not that it would matter 'cause
12   I can't read on an empty stomach and I don't even *smell* my
13   muffin yet and by the way has my mother called yet this
14   morning?
15   GRAHAM: No, sir. Are you expecting her to?
16   BOSS: None of your business but if you must know I haven't
17   gotten a birthday card from her yet and I'm convinced that
18   she's forgotten me again — *What on earth is taking so long*
19   *with my muffin?!*
20   MORGAN: It's almost ready, sir. I think we need a microwave toaster
21   oven. *(Laughs, but he's the only one.)* So it's your birthday?
22   BOSS: Of course not, you idiot — do you think I'd be here on my
23   birthday? It's the middle of next month but if it doesn't get here
24   today wire her to remind her that her only son has gotten a year
25   older and his own mother doesn't even care! *(Slams the door.)*
26   GRAHAM: *(Pause as they look at each other.)* You know, he has
27   issues ...
28   MORGAN: Issues? That's like saying Hitler was a little mean ...
29   GRAHAM: Hey, Morgan, I didn't see you at Sunday school
30   last week.
31   MORGAN: No, I had to miss. The kids were both sick. Was it good?
32   GRAHAM: Oh, yeah! We talked about God's mercy. You know,
33   how patient he is with us, even though we mess up sometimes.
34   MORGAN: Man, isn't that the truth. I don't know where I would
35   be without that kind of grace!

1   GRAHAM: Me neither. It's pretty amazing when you think about
2   the kind of patience it must take to be able to overlook some
3   of the stuff we put God through.
4   MORGAN: Yeah, really. I just wish we could get old Mr. Finkel-
5   heimer to come to church. He could use a few lessons on
6   patience!
7   GRAHAM: Shhh! Here he comes!
8   BOSS: Never mind the Mayer report — I've already rewritten it!
9   GRAHAM: Sir, your muffin is …
10   BOSS: Never mind the muffin either I'm on my way to lunch and
11   don't worry about that call from my mother I've already
12   taken care of it and she *had* forgotten even though she said
13   that she hadn't and that she was going to drop a card in the
14   mail tomorrow — If I get any calls I'll be at that new Japan-
15   ese fast food restaurant up the street at one of their standing
16   tables but if you're not back from lunch by the time I get back,
17   then you're both fired!
18   MORGAN: But, sir, it's only 9:05!
19   BOSS: *(Pause)* Your point?
20   MORGAN: *(Caught off-guard)* Oh, nothing …
21   GRAHAM: *(Holding out mug)* Your coffee, sir?
22   BOSS: Forget it! I'll be done with lunch before it cools — I'll have
23   it when I get back along with the Shrock report if you know
24   what's good for you! *(Slams the door on the other side or walks*
25   *out briskly.)*
26   MORGAN: *(Looking at GRAHAM, who is looking at him.)* You were
27   saying?
28   GRAHAM: The man has issues, *and* a caffeine problem.
29   MORGAN: *(Moving toward the door)* So, join me for a quick lunch?
30   GRAHAM: Who eats at nine in the morning?
31   MORGAN: We do. We'll grab a bagel or something. When he's in
32   this kind of a mood, you just roll with it.
33   GRAHAM: But what happens at noon, when I get hungry?
34   MORGAN: We'll go to lunch then. At the rate he's traveling, the
35   work day will be over by ten thirty.

1   GRAHAM: Oh, yeah! *(Pause)* I just remembered why we put up
2   with him!
3   MORGAN: Exactly, my patient friend. Join me?
4   GRAHAM: After you, oh wise one! *(They exit quickly.)*
5
6
7
8
9
10
11
12
13
14
15
16
17
18
19
20
21
22
23
24
25
26
27
28
29
30
31
32
33
34
35

When I Remember Dad ...

A sketch about fatherhood.

Theme: Father's Day

**Scripture
Reference:**   Ephesians 6:2-4

Synopsis: A couple of vignettes in the life of a dad demonstrate the humorous foibles common to fathers everywhere. The real trademark of a committed dad is his love for his children.

Cast: Narrator
Dad
Dan

Props: None.

**Sound
Effects:**   Dog yelping.

Setting: At home to start, then on the road. Place two chairs side by side for a "car."

1   *(NARRATOR is off to one side at a lectern. DAD and DAN may*
2   *freeze in a pose, with DAD pointing and DAN looking, until DAD*
3   *says his first line.)*
4   NARRATOR: I guess when I remember Dad, I think of a lot of
5   things. I remember the way my father was never satisfied with
6   the way other people used to do things. "If you want something
7   done right ..." he would say. And then he would find the most
8   difficult, creative way of doing it ... eventually. Like the time
9   my sisters wanted a dollhouse for their Barbies ...
10   DAD: Look at this, Danny — it's a Barbie high-rise condo!
11   DAN: You built this? I thought you were just going to buy one.
12   DAD: I was. But you wouldn't believe the cheap plastic stuff that
13   they're selling nowadays! Feel this! *(Mimes knocking on the out-*
14   *side of the dollhouse.)* Solid three-quarter-inch plywood
15   construction.
16   DAN: *(Looking closer.)* Wow. The inside looks really nice, too. Even
17   the refrigerator looks realistic.
18   DAD: That's not the half of it! *(Reaches into the tiny kitchen and pulls*
19   *the door on the refrigerator open.)*
20   DAN: Wow! A light in the fridge goes on when you open the door?
21   Dad, this thing is huge!
22   DAD: Six stories.
23   DAN: Isn't that a bit much?
24   DAD: Not when you have ... *(Pulls out a remote control)* a super-
25   deluxe remote-control elevator! *(DAD and DAN freeze.)*
26   NARRATOR: Which explains why the house he started to remodel
27   in 1970 was finally completed in 1986. But that was my dad.
28   He worked from sunup until sundown, always looking for a
29   new challenge. When I was fifteen, I uh ... finally was able to
30   give him one ...
31   DAD: All right, remember everything I told you. Depress the clutch,
32   pump the gas once, turn the key, and put your foot on the
33   brake. All right, now, look behind you to see if the way is clear.
34   Not in the mirror! Never trust the mirror! Always look over
35   your right shoulder to see if the way is clear. *(He does.)* Now,

1   turn your wheel to the right, slowly ... slowly. Now ease your
2   way out into traffic.
3 DAN: But Dad, you always just ...
4 DAD: Do as I say, not as I do.
5 DAN: OK.
6 DAD: OK. Keep your hands at ten and two o'clock on the wheel.
7   Your eyes should be scanning everything, but mostly the road
8   ahead. Never, ever take your eyes off the road.
9 DAN: But Dad, remember that time that you were reading the
10   paper on the way to Abilene ...
11 DAD: Do as I say, not as I do.
12 DAN: Right.
13 DAD: You're going a bit fast — slow it down, we're in no hurry.
14   Hands still at ten and two. Don't follow so close — that car
15   ahead could stop at any time. Always drive defensively — the
16   other guy is always going to do something stupid. Don't make
17   any unnecessary moves on the road — stay in one lane ...
18 DAN: But you always pass on the right when ...
19 DAD: Do you want to learn how to drive or not?
20 DAN: Do as you say, not as you do.
21 DAD: Correct. Hands at ten and two ... *(DAD and DAN freeze.)*
22 NARRATOR: But I eventually learned how to drive anyway. I took
23   my driver's test in my father's 1974 Volkswagen bus. I
24   remember the instructor saying, "If you can pass the test in
25   this, you should be able to drive anything!" That was another
26   thing about my dad. He wasn't a professing tightwad, but he
27   loved their economics. If there was ever anything that he
28   couldn't do himself for less money, it didn't need to be done.
29   He could do anything himself, from masonry to carpentry to
30   dentistry. He was a mechanic, an inventor, and on one ill-fated
31   afternoon, a veterinarian. *(DAD walks across the stage, calling,*
32   *"Here kitty, kitty, kitty!")* You see, Mom had finally laid down
33   the law about taking the animals to the vet to get them
34   neutered. *(DAD walks across stage, whistling for the dog.)* At
35   thirty dollars apiece, no less. Well, that was far too much. And

1. Dad, being the avid reader that he was, had just stumbled
2. across a do-it-yourself neutering article in the latest issue of
3. *Too Much Time on Your Hands* quarterly.
4. DAD: *(Walks across the stage, calling)* Come here, guys! I've got
5. something for you!
6. NARRATOR: Suffice to say, the animals didn't come near Dad for
7. almost two years. *("Yipe, yipe, yipe!" is heard in the back-*
8. *ground.)* But the thing I think about the most is that Dad had
9. a never-ending love for kids. There were four of us in the
10. family, but my parents were also foster parents for nearly
11. thirty other kids over an eight-year stretch of time. I think
12. "Suffer the little children to come unto me" (Mark 10:14, KJV)
13. is probably Dad's favorite verse, because he doesn't just read
14. it, he lives it. As busy as I remember my father being, I still
15. remember him taking time out to toss a Frisbee around with
16. me or to take us down to the river to hike, or just to play
17. games at the kitchen table. Now that I have a child of my own,
18. I look back on those times with fondness and hope. Hope that
19. I can do the same kinds of things that he did to instill fond
20. memories in us. And as right as my dad was most of the time,
21. he may have been wrong about one thing. At times it's best to
22. do as he does, not necessarily as he says.
23.
24.
25.
26.
27.
28.
29.
30.
31.
32.
33.
34.
35.

When We All Work Together...

A sketch about our need for each other.

Theme: Cooperation, body of Christ

**Scripture
Reference:**   1 Corinthians 12:4-27

Synopsis: Two characters, one representing music and one representing words, both claim to be the superior mode of communication. Eventually, both see their need for the other.

Cast: Music
Words

Props: None.

Setting: A debate. You may place two lecterns facing each other at an angle (inverted V) so the characters face each other, yet are still visible to the audience.

1   *(Two characters, WORDS and MUSIC, enter from opposite sides*
2   *and take their places, as in a debate.)*
3   MUSIC: I am music. I am clearly the most eloquent form of com-
4   munication ever created.
5   WORDS: Ha. I am words. Without me there would be no commu-
6   nication.
7   MUSIC: Music embodies feelings, emotions. Music can create a mood.
8   WORDS: Words are very clear, very logical. You can explain exactly
9   what you mean with words, so there is no confusion.
10   MUSIC: Music soothes the savage beast. Music is calming, good for
11   the soul. Without music, who could think clearly enough to
12   compose a sentence?
13   WORDS: Without words, there would be chaos. There would be no
14   laws, no rules, no order. Without words, we couldn't collect
15   our thoughts and express them to others.
16   MUSIC: Music is the language of the heart. While there are many
17   languages and most people only understand one or two, every-
18   one understands music. It is universal.
19   WORDS: Music is too vague, too ambiguous. Sometimes it's even
20   confusing.
21   MUSIC: Words are boring and flat. They're emotionless.
22   WORDS: Without words, you wouldn't have even been able to
23   communicate that.
24   MUSIC: Words are only good for giving orders, for making people
25   angry. The tongue is a vile weapon.
26   WORDS: Oh, yeah? Words can also say I'm sorry. Or I love you.
27   Or tell others how much you appreciate them ...
28   MUSIC: Music lets a lot of people work together, like in a symphony.
29   Only one person can talk at a time or it gets too confusing.
30   WORDS: Oh, yeah? Well, I got a few words for you!
31   MUSIC: Oh, yeah? Well, bring 'em on, buddy! I'm gonna blast you
32   away with a big band tune!
33   SONG LEADER: Hey, hey! You two just calm down a minute.
34   Don't you think you could come together and recognize that
35   you can both play an important role together?

1   **MUSIC and WORDS:** *(Together)* **Really? How?**
2   **SONG LEADER: How about a song?** *(MUSIC and WORDS exit as*
3   *SONG LEADER or worship team comes forward for the next song.)*
4
5
6
7
8
9
10
11
12
13
14
15
16
17
18
19
20
21
22
23
24
25
26
27
28
29
30
31
32
33
34
35

Who's in Control Here?

A sketch about internal versus external control.

Theme: Control, consistency, self-control

Scripture References: Joshua 24:15, 2 Peter 1:6

Synopsis: A teacher thinks his class is the most well-behaved ever, but mayhem breaks out whenever his back is turned.

Cast: Teacher
Visitor
Student 1
Student 2
Student 3
Student extras (optional)

Props: Paper for notes and paperwads, textbooks, pencils.

Setting: A classroom. Place four or five desks or chairs at Center Stage and turned around, so the students' backs are toward the audience.

1   *(The TEACHER is in front of the class, facing the audience. The*

2   *STUDENTS sit in their desks or chairs, facing the TEACHER so*

3   *that only their backs are seen by the audience. The VISITOR*

4   *stands beside the TEACHER.)*

5   **TEACHER: Good morning, class!**

6   **ALL:** *(Sarcastically sweet)* **Good morning, Mr. Hemplebert!**

7   **TEACHER:** *(To the VISITOR)* **You will be so glad you chose to**

8   **observe this particular class.**

9   **VISITOR: Oh? Why is that?**

10   **TEACHER: This class is the one that I have placed the most rules**

11   **upon, and they have responded beautifully. They are my pride**

12   **and joy. See how well-behaved they are?**

13   **VISITOR: They do seem well-behaved.**

14   **TEACHER: Oh, yes! You will do well to watch and learn.** *(To the*

15   *Class)* **Class, today we have a visitor. This is Mr. Williams**

16   **from the University. He is here to observe what a well-disci-**

17   **plined class looks like. Say hello, class.**

18   **ALL:** *(Still sarcastically sweet)* **Hello, Mr. Williams!**

19   **VISITOR: Hello, class.**

20   **TEACHER: Now, I thought we would start off by reviewing the**

21   **rules of our classroom so that Mr. Williams can see why you**

22   **are such a wonderful class. Who can tell me rule number one?**

23   *(All raise hands. TEACHER calls on one.)* **Yes, Johnny?**

24   **STUDENT 1: Always pay attention.**

25   **TEACHER: Very good! Now let's just write these up on the board,**

26   **shall we?** *(He turns his back and pantomimes writing the rule on*

27   *the board. As he turns around, the class quietly begins to whisper*

28   *to each other, turn around in their seats, pass notes, etc. As soon*

29   *as the teacher turns back around, they are perfectly facing the*

30   *front again, hands folded together on their desks. The VISITOR*

31   *observes all this. TEACHER turns around.)* **Now, who can tell me**

32   **the second rule of our room?** *(Chooses one of the raised hands.)*

33   **Yes, Tessa?**

34   **STUDENT 2: Never disturb others with foolish behavior.**

35   **TEACHER: Excellent!** *(Turns to write the rule on the board as before,*

1   *repeating the rule as he writes it on the board. As he does so, the*
2   *entire class is throwing paperwads and pencils at one another as*
3   *if to mock the rule. When he finishes and turns around, again,*
4   *they are angelic.)* **All right, who can tell me rule number three?**
5   *(Again all hands are up and he chooses one.)* **Yes, Bartholomew?**
6   **STUDENT 3: Always take turns and raise your hand.**
7   **TEACHER: That's right!** *(Turns to write and all the kids start push-*
8   *ing STUDENT 3 because they thought they should have been*
9   *called upon. The TEACHER hears the disturbance and without*
10   *turning around, says:)* **I hear a murmur ...** *(The class quiets*
11   *down but still picks on STUDENT 3 until the TEACHER turns*
12   *around. Then they are angelic again.)*
13   **TEACHER: And what happens when we break these rules?**
14   **ALL: We go to Mr. Feinstein's office!**
15   **TEACHER: All right, class, now let's begin our lesson.** *(TEACHER*
16   *turns to the VISITOR. The class once again begins their rowdy*
17   *behavior, quietly.)* **Now, Mr. Williams, you didn't say which**
18   **class you were observing for. Psychology? Sociology?**
19   **VISITOR:** *(Loudly, so the class can hear)* **Actually, Mr. Hemplebert,**
20   **I'm not here from the University.**
21   **TEACHER: Oh?**
22   **VISITOR: I'm going to be the summer school teacher, and I**
23   **thought I'd get an idea of the kids that I'll be teaching by**
24   **coming in here, since your whole class will probably be taking**
25   **it.** *(The kids all stop their movements simultaneously and look at*
26   *the VISITOR.)* **Unless, of course, they show remarkable**
27   **improvement.**
28   **TEACHER: I see. Well, make yourself comfortable.**
29   **VISITOR: Thank you.**
30   **TEACHER: All right, class, are we ready to begin?** *(The class, still*
31   *frozen, suddenly lunges under their seats for their books and*
32   *quickly open them, ready to begin.)* **Excellent. Now our lesson**
33   **today ...** *(Fade)*
34
35

The Wide Road

A monolog about "that place."

Theme: Hell

Scripture References: Matthew 7:13-14, 2 Thessalonians 1:7-9

Synopsis: Satan welcomes the latest tour bus full of passengers to hell, where he points out the various "attractions." This is a place no one wants to be — and it's forever.

Cast: Satan

Props: Microphone.

Setting: Hell. Optional: a sign that reads "Welcome to hell!" with a smiley face on it, or "Have a nice day! (Just kidding!)"

1   *(SATAN stands at Center Stage with a microphone as the monolog*
2   *begins.)*
3   SATAN: OK, welcome again, all of you! What a good-looking
4   group! Well, allow me to introduce myself again. My name is
5   Satan, but you may recognize me as Mephistopheles, the
6   Prince of Darkness, Lord of the Underworld, etc., and I'll be
7   your tour guide for ... well ... eternity, I guess, so sit back,
8   relax and try to enjoy yourselves as much as that's possible.
9   As we approach the gates of hell, I'd like to direct your
10   attention to the beverage cart in the middle of the aisle.
11   *(Pause)* What's that? Yes, of course I'm kidding, you moron!
12   You expect we'd have what — ice water, perhaps? All right,
13   this illustrates a very important point. You're obviously not a
14   very bright group, or else you wouldn't be here, but in order
15   not to waste my time, please refrain from comments like,
16   "There must be some mistake," or "Can I have another
17   chance?" It's a waste of time, and I won't stand for it. If you
18   feel like you've been wronged, you may speak to an attorney.
19   By the way, you'll each be rooming with one. *(Pause)* Because
20   this is hell, that's why! And besides, we have way too many of
21   them down here as well, so get used to it!
22   *(Pause, then loudly)* All right! Simmer down! *(Pause again)*
23   Heh-heh! I love saying that! OK, now if I could direct your
24   attention to the road we're on, have you happened to notice
25   how smooth the ride is? This particular highway is paved with
26   the finest of intentions as wide as the eye can see. Off to your
27   left, you'll notice the final exit before the actual gates, a
28   straight, narrow path that is very steep and rocky. Ironically,
29   in just a few short minutes, you'll wish we would've taken it
30   instead. Alas, at this point? Not an option. *(Laughing to him-*
31   *self)* But if it's any consolation, your ride has been much more
32   comfortable. But you already knew that! That's why you're
33   on this tour! *(Pause)*
34   And now, as we enter the gates, I know that most of you
35   came with a great deal of baggage; for those of you who have

1	not yet attempted to store it in the overhead bins, please don't
2	waste your time. You'll carry burdens with you from this point
3	forward anyway. *(Pause)* You'll notice that there is no waiting
4	at our gates — there never is. It's as easy to get in as it is
5	impossible to get out. Take a long, last look at the gates, it's
6	the last time you'll see them from the outside.
7	*(Pause, then loudly)* **Please, people! I may be the author of**
8	**confusion, but there are limits! All right. Now, if I could have**
9	**your attention, I'd like you to look at the lake of fire on the**
10	**right. Please take note of the "No Fishing" signs which have**
11	**been posted at various intervals around the perimeter. Please**
12	**also note that while we do not allow boating, swimming is**
13	**allowed and even highly encouraged. And for those of you who**
14	**enjoy sunbathing, you may do so on any side of the lake, but**
15	**we highly recommend using a sunblock of two million or**
16	**better, which is available at the gift shop. Now —** *(Pauses, as if*
17	*he has been interrupted.)* **Yes?** *(Pause)* **Ice fishing in the winter?**
18	*(Rolls his eyes sarcastically.)* **Yes, sir, I suppose you could.**
19	**When the lake freezes over.** *(Pause, rolling his eyes again)*
20	Now, where was I? Oh, yes — I know that many of you
21	asked about smoking earlier; you may smoke. In fact, you will
22	probably all smoke. It's inevitable, really. *(Pause)* Now, over
23	on your left, you'll notice an endless expanse of brimstone
24	quarries — each of you will be quite familiar with these over
25	the rest of your stay here. This is where you will work for the
26	rest of eternity.
27	Now before we go on, is anybody too warm in here? *(Pause)*
28	OK, those of you who raised you hands, you are obviously the
29	leaders. Too stupid to deal with, but leaders nonetheless. I'm
30	going to ask you to help organize the others when we begin to
31	disembark the bus. Thank you! Just over here at the top of the
32	hill, you'll notice a very large building with no windows. This
33	is the dormitory where you will be staying.
34	OK, I know you're all a little surprised to be here, so first
35	of all, don't worry about it. You have an eternity to get used to

1	the idea. There are a few rules, but the handbook would take
2	you a little longer than eternity to read, so I'll make it easy for
3	you. As your brochure told you, we are very accommodating
4	here in hades. It will be a different experience for each of you,
5	but a few things will be constant. You will notice that the disco
6	accordion Muzak has been pumped into each of your rooms.
7	Also, there will be daily algebraic story problems, and you are
8	now on an all-bran diet. Outside of these things, all the ques-
9	tions you may have will be answered by my mime assistants
10	later on at the reception. As we pull into the parking lot,
11	please take all of your baggage and step off the bus. I have a
12	burning desire to get reacquainted with each of you later!
13	*(Exits.)*
14	
15	
16	
17	
18	
19	
20	
21	
22	
23	
24	
25	
26	
27	
28	
29	
30	
31	
32	
33	
34	
35	

A Wretch Like Me

A sketch extolling God's mercy.

Theme: Guilt, mercy

**Scripture
References:** 1 Timothy 1:12-17, Hebrews 10:17

Synopsis: One person climbs out on the roof with thoughts of ending it all because she is so sinful. Another person convinces her to give God's forgiveness a try.

Cast: Person 1
Person 2

Props: None.

Setting: The roof ledge of a building.

1   *(PERSON 1 stands on the roof of a building, supposedly wracked*
2   *with guilt and contemplating injury to herself. Then PERSON 2*
3   *climbs out via any opening in a curtain or by an imagined win-*
4   *dow to talk her out of it. The feeling of being up on a roof may be*
5   *accomplished by having both characters press their bodies up*
6   *against a wall as if they were on a ledge, or by edging their way*
7   *along a top step with their backs against an imaginary wall.)*
8   **PERSON 2: Mind if I come outside to join you?**
9   **PERSON 1:** *(Pauses apathetically.)* **I guess. It's a free country.**
10   **PERSON 2:** *(Pantomimes climbing through a window and edges his*
11   *way to where PERSON 1 stands. After getting a bit closer,*
12   *PERSON 2 asks:)* **What are you doing out here?**
13   **PERSON 1: What does it look like I'm doing?**
14   **PERSON 2: Well, it looks as though you've climbed out onto a**
15   **window ledge ...**
16   **PERSON 1: You're brilliant! Now go back inside before you fall,**
17   **and leave me alone.**
18   **PERSON 2: Well, I would, but I'm a little worried about why you**
19   **would climb out here.**
20   **PERSON 1: Look, Einstein, isn't it obvious? I'm sick of my life and**
21   **the way I keep messing it up and I came out here so I could**
22   **end it all!**
23   **PERSON 2: Oh, man, you can't do that!**
24   **PERSON 1: Sure I can. No one will even miss me.**
25   **PERSON 2: No, I mean you can't kill yourself.**
26   **PERSON 1: You don't think I have the guts?**
27   **PERSON 2: No, it's not that. It's just that this is only a second story**
28   **window. We're barely high enough for you to break your ankle.**
29   **PERSON 1:** *(Pause)* **Well, have you ever broken an ankle? It could**
30   **get infected and then I'd die.**
31   **PERSON 2: I think the paramedics would ...**
32   **PERSON 1: Look, what's your point?**
33   **PERSON 2: Well, since you obviously didn't come out here to kill**
34   **yourself, I thought you might like to talk about it.**
35   **PERSON 1: Well, I don't.**

1   PERSON 2: Come on ...

2   PERSON 1: *(Pause)* Oh, you don't care.

3   PERSON 2: Try me.

4   PERSON 1: *(Pause)* Well, it's just that I'm an awful person. A sinner,
5   you know?

6   PERSON 2: Yeah, I think I can relate.

7   PERSON 1: I mean, I just can't seem to stop doing the things that
8   I know I shouldn't do. You know?

9   PERSON 2: Yeah. I do that all the time too.

10   PERSON 1: You do? *(Pause)* But I thought you were a really good
11   Christian.

12   PERSON 2: Well, I *am* a Christian. But that doesn't mean I don't
13   mess up. Every day.

14   PERSON 1: Really? But how can you be a Christian if you sin
15   every day?

16   PERSON 2: Simple, really. I'm human. Just like you. And God
17   knows that. He forgives us when we mess things up.

18   PERSON 1: But every day? What's the point of even trying?

19   PERSON 2: Well, I guess it's the fact that we *do* keep trying that
20   makes forgiveness work so well.

21   PERSON 1: What do you mean?

22   PERSON 2: Well, take Paul — in the Bible. He started off killing
23   Christians until God showed him that what he was doing was
24   wrong. Then he changed his ways and became one of them. And
25   even after that, he still made mistakes. But he kept trying, and
26   God kept forgiving him.

27   PERSON 1: Wow. I've never killed anybody. I've wanted to a
28   couple of times, but ...

29   PERSON 2: God knows that we're not always going to be able to
30   live the way that we want to. But he has so much grace that
31   when we do something wrong, and then we ask him to take
32   away our guilt, he doesn't even remember our sin.

33   PERSON 1: Wait a minute. God forgets?

34   PERSON 2: That's what it says in Hebrews.

35   PERSON 1: What if I remind him? Like, a lot?

1   PERSON 2: By sinning again? It doesn't matter. That's how
2   merciful he is. If you are truly sorry, he remembers it no more.
3   PERSON 1: Wow! I guess that means there's nothing I've done that
4   I can't ask God to help me get past.
5   PERSON 2: Now you're getting it!
6   PERSON 1: Boy, do I feel stupid. Sorry to make you come out here
7   and everything.
8   PERSON 2: Don't mention it. I needed the fresh air break. Does
9   this mean you're ready to come back inside?
10 PERSON 1: Yeah, I think so. Thanks for talking with me.
11 PERSON 2: What are friends for? *(They both rise to move inside,*
12   *PERSON 1 going first and PERSON 2 following. PERSON 1*
13   *turns her head to talk to PERSON 2 as they move inside.)*
14 PERSON 1: You know, I really could have broken my ankle, gotten
15   a staph infection, and died.
16 PERSON 2: Oh, I'm sure.
17 PERSON 1: *(Pause)* You sure you forgive me?
18 PERSON 2: Forgive you for what? *(They both exit.)*
19
20
21
22
23
24
25
26
27
28
29
30
31
32
33
34
35

You Be the Judge!

A sketch looking at the consequences of judging others.

Theme: Judging others

**Scripture
References:** Matthew 7:1-6, 13:40-49, 16:27; Acts 11:2-18

Synopsis: Three game show contestants are quick to judge others' situations as sinful without knowing all the facts. Consequently, no one wins.

Cast: Narrator
Sonny
Phil
Dottie
Chris

Props: Three cards, three markers, three hand-held buzzers. (Use buzzers that come with board games. If they are unavailable, the players can simply make a buzzing sound.)

**Sound
Effects:** Buzzer (this is in addition to the hand-held buzzers and is heard over the PA system when the judges deem an answer wrong), organ accompaniment playing something reminiscent of a game show theme, and clock-type music (music is optional.) It is also helpful to

have some people scattered through the congregation to instigate cheering and other audience responses.

Setting: A stereotypical game show set. Set up a podium for Sonny and three chairs or podiums for the contestants.

1   *(The three CONTESTANTS — PHIL, DOTTIE and CHRIS — are*
2   *seated in their chairs, waiting for the show to start. If possible,*
3   *musical accompaniment that sounds like a game show theme may*
4   *be playing in the background.)*
5 NARRATOR: *(From Off-stage)* **And now, it's time once again for**
6   **everybody's favorite game show, *You be the Judge!* And here's**
7   **the host of our show, Mr. Sonny Weathers!** *(SONNY comes*
8   *running out to the applause of his adoring public, smiling his false*
9   *smile and waving. On-stage CONTESTANTS all clap and cheer*
10   *wildly.)*
11 SONNY: **Thank you all, and welcome once again to the world's**
12   **most imitated and popular show, *You Be the Judge!* where our**
13   **contestants try to figure out whether their neighbors are**
14   **committing sinful acts or not. As always, please feel free to**
15   **play along at home — after all, that's the fun part! All right,**
16   **are we ready to play?** *(All CONTESTANTS look at each other*
17   *happily and nod, mumble "Yeah!" or "You bet!")* **First of all,**
18   **let's meet our contestants, shall we?** *(Walks over to CONTES-*
19   *TANTS.)* **Our first contestant is a Sunday school teacher from**
20   **Peoria, Illinois. Please welcome Mr. Phil Peerless!** *(Cheering)*
21   **Mr. Peerless, do you think you know a little about sinful acts?**
22 PHIL: **Well, sure — other people's!**
23 SONNY: **All righty!** *(Pause)* **Our next contestant comes to us from**
24   **Bangor, Maine. She's an elder in her home church, and her**
25   **name is Dottie Dooright!** *(Cheering)* **Ms. Dooright.** *(Pause)* **So**
26   **your church has ... lady elders?**
27 DOTTIE: **Why, yes, Sonny. I've been an elder for the last two years.**
28 SONNY: **Interesting! I've never thought women should be leaders**
29   **in the church. Seems a little too ... modern for me!**
30 DOTTIE: **What? Why shouldn't women be allowed to be leaders?**
31 SONNY: **Okey-dokey! Moving right along! Our third contestant**
32   **today is Mr. Chris Ideal, from Pocatello, Idaho!** *(Cheering)* **Mr.**
33   **Ideal, it says here you're a lay leader. What does that entail?**
34 CHRIS: **Well, Sonny, I'm very involved in my church. I've served on**
35   **many committees, including our last pastoral search committee.**

1   SONNY: OOOOH! I'll bet that was fun! Tell me about it.
2   CHRIS: You bet! Why, we got to disqualify one candidate because
3   we didn't like the way he dressed!
4   SONNY: Makes perfect sense to me!
5   CHRIS: But I should say, in Ms. Dooright's defense, that our
6   church also has women as elders ...
7   SONNY: *(Extremely bored)* Whatever! Let's play our game! *(Runs*
8   *back over to his podium.)* All right, contestants, you know how
9   to play. I'll give you a scenario, and you buzz in and tell me
10   whether you think the person in the scenario has committed a
11   sinful act by saying either "Sinful" or "Not sinful." Got it? *(All*
12   *nod.)* Now, we'll start off with a few easy ones to get you into
13   the swing of things. All righty — hands on buzzers. The first
14   scenario is: You are driving to church on Sunday. You see a
15   man mowing his lawn near ...
16   DOTTIE: *(Buzzes.)* Sinful! *(A buzzer sounds.)*
17   SONNY: Oh, I'm sorry! The answer was "Not sinful!" It seems the
18   man was a Seventh-day Adventist!
19   DOTTIE:So? I still think it's sinful because the Sabbath is on Sunday!
20   SONNY: Judges? *(Buzzer sounds again.)* Oooh, sorry! One of our
21   judges is also a Seventh-day Adventist! Next question —
22   hands on buzzers. This woman had a family of five to support
23   and skipped her tithe for three months so she could ...
24   PHIL: *(Buzzes.)* Sinful! *(A buzzer sounds.)*
25   SONNY: Ooooh, sorry, Phil! The correct answer was "Not sinful."
26   It was to pay for a pair of shoes so that her son could go to
27   Sunday school, and ironically enough, that woman was your
28   mother. *(Awwww! heard from the audience.)*
29   PHIL: Mommy?
30   SONNY: Next question. This person is one of the wealthiest people
31   around, yet, as a successful game show host, has never once
32   tithed ten percent to his church, often only has time for God
33   on holidays, and belittles his contestants' views without
34   regard for their feelings because he thinks they're all a bunch
35   of losers. *(Pause, as everyone realizes that it is SONNY, but no*

1   *one wants to buzz in. After looking at each other, CHRIS buzzes*
2   *in.)*
3   **SONNY: Yes, Chris?**
4   **CHRIS:** *(Hesitantly)* **Not sinful?** *(A buzzer sounds.)*
5   **SONNY: Oooh, no, I'm sorry — the correct answer was "sinful as**
6   **all get out!"** *(Pause)* **Remember, contestants, kissing up to the**
7   **host and excusing his behavior does not make it right! All**
8   **right, last question for this round! A person is seen with a**
9   **woman of ill-repute in a seedy part of town ...**
10 **PHIL: Sinful!** *(Buzzer sounds.)* **Oh, man!**
11 **SONNY: Ooooh, sorry! That was the pastor of the rescue mission!**
12   *(Pause)* **All right, it seems as though we have no score heading**
13   **into the Final Judgment round. According to our rules, that**
14   **means that the person who gets this question right is automat-**
15   **ically our champion. And what does our champion win, Bob?**
16 **NARRATOR:** *(From Off-stage)* **That's right, Sonny! Our winner**
17   **today will receive an all-expenses-paid trip for two to the**
18   **Glass Cathedral in sunny California, where they will each be**
19   **able to throw one stone.** *(Pause for laughter)* **And then it's off**
20   **to Disneyland! Sonny?**
21 **SONNY: All right, contestants, remember that this is for the game.**
22   **I'll give you a scenario, and you write down either sinful or**
23   **not sinful. Everybody ready? OK! This person, supposedly a**
24   **religious man, was arrested and convicted of breaking several**
25   **laws, including working on the Sabbath, blasphemy, vandalism**
26   **of a church, and disrupting the peace, among other things. He**
27   **is sentenced to capital punishment, mostly because of the**
28   **blasphemy part. Sinful or not sinful?** *(All CONTESTANTS*
29   *appear to be writing down their answers as some clock-type music*
30   *plays in the background. After a ten second pause ...)* **Okey-**
31   **dokey! We'll start with Chris.** *(CHRIS holds up a card that says*
32   *"sinful.")* **All right, how about you, Phil?** *(Holds up a sign that*
33   *says, "sinful.")* **Okey-dokey. And you, Dottie?** *(Holds up a sign*
34   *that says, "sinful.")* **All right. Well, it seems the**
35   **correct answer was "not sinful," as the person we were talking**

1　about is Jesus Christ. I'm afraid no one wins! *(Everybody is*
2　*visibly disappointed.)* Looks like Bob and I are heading to Dis-
3　neyland again! As a consolation to our contestants, however,
4　I'd like to refer to Matthew 7:1 and 2. If we followed the scrip-
5　tural premise in these verses, "Judge not that ye be not
6　judged. For as you do, you will also be judged in the same
7　manner," (Author's paraphrase) we would put you all to death!
8　*(CONTESTANTS stop complaining and look at each other, fright-*
9　*ened.)* Tune in next time for *You Be the Judge!* Good-bye,
10　everybody!
11
12
13
14
15
16
17
18
19
20
21
22
23
24
25
26
27
28
29
30
31
32
33
34
35

The Zoo Tour

A sketch on respecting differences.

Theme: Prejudice, diversity, tolerance

**Scripture
References:** Mark 6:2-3, Galatians 3:28

Synopsis: A group of visitors to the zoo is less than enthusiastic when every exhibit contains the same species of animal. What a boring world it would be if we were all the same!

Cast: Guide
Visitor 1
Visitor 2
Visitor 3
Visitor 4
Visitor 5
Visitor extras (optional)

Props: None.

Setting: A zoo.

1   *(A tour GUIDE is very methodically, but with some enthusiasm,*
2   *directing a tour of the animals. A crowd of VISITORS follows him,*
3   *looking around as a tour group usually does, but following the*
4   *GUIDE's pantomiming as he wanders about the stage, pointing*
5   *out the various exhibits.)*
6   **GUIDE: Now, here we have the exotic brown bear. The brown bear**
7   **is indigenous to the northwest United States and Canada.**
8   **VISITORS:** *(Make oohing and aahing noises.)*
9   **GUIDE: And over here we have the brown bear. There are approx-**
10 **imately nine hundred brown bears currently in captivity.**
11 *(VISITORS are somewhat less than enthusiastic, looking around*
12 *at each other a little bit as if to see if they are the only ones who*
13 *find two consecutive brown bear exhibits unusual.)* **And if you'll**
14 **direct your attention to the exhibit behind you, you'll notice**
15 **one of our premier attractions.** *Two* **brown bears. The zoo is**
16 **currently hoping that these particular animals will find each**
17 **other attractive enough so that if you come back again next**
18 **year, we'll have a wonderful addition to our zoo. Now, if you'll**
19 **follow me over this way, we'll proceed to our bear exhibits.**
20 *(VISITORS begin to murmur to themselves a bit but follow any-*
21 *way, hoping that maybe this exhibit will hold a different type of*
22 *bear. After a brief pause, the GUIDE continues.)* **This is my**
23 **favorite selection of animals at the zoo, and I believe you'll**
24 **find them to be your favorites as well. Here we have a brown**
25 **bear ...** *(As he speaks, the VISITORS chime in on the words*
26 *"brown bear." GUIDE responds.)* **Oh! I can see you folks have**
27 **taken the tour before!**
28 **VISITOR 1: Excuse me, but do you have any other animals at this**
29 **particular zoo?**
30 **GUIDE: Well, of course! It is a zoo, after all. In fact, we've just**
31 *barely* **begun our tour.**
32 **VISITOR 1: Uh, yes. Well, what I meant was, do you have anything**
33 **besides brown bears?**
34 **GUIDE: What are you getting at?**
35 **VISITOR 1: I mean, are there any other animals here?**

1   GUIDE: You don't like brown bears? What kind of a person
2   are you?
3   VISITOR 1: No, no. I like bears. I just want to know if there are any
4   other animals besides bears.
5   GUIDE: Brown bears.
6   VISITOR 1: Yes, yes! Are there?
7   GUIDE: Sir *(or Ma'am)*, with all due respect, you are holding up
8   our tour. These people would like to see the rest of the animals
9   in the zoo!
10   VISITOR 2: Well, actually, I think the rest of us would like to know
11   whether or not there are other animals, too, right? *(VISITORS*
12   *verbalize that they would by murmuring and nodding among*
13   *themselves.)*
14   VISITOR 3: So are there?
15   GUIDE: All right now, calm down! Let's proceed with the tour!
16   *(Regaining composure.)* Now, over here we have ... *(Pause)* a
17   polar bear with a large brown birthmark.
18   VISITOR 4: That's not a polar bear!
19   GUIDE: Oh, yes it is.
20   VISITOR 3: No, it's not! Polar bears are white!
21   GUIDE: Look at his ear! Completely white!
22   VISITOR 2: That's dust! He's completely brown!
23   GUIDE: Look. Who's the guide here?
24   VISITOR 1: Listen. Do you have any other animals here or not?
25   GUIDE: Yes, of course!
26   VISITOR 3: That aren't brown bears?
27   GUIDE: *What is wrong with brown bears?!*
28   VISITOR 1: Nothing! But there are other animals.
29   GUIDE: *(Mumbling)* Not at *this* zoo ...
30   VISITORS: What?
31   GUIDE: *(Louder)* I said, not at *this* zoo!
32   VISITOR 4: But doesn't that get boring?
33   GUIDE: The brown bear is everything you could want in an
34   animal! They're big and cuddly and strong and gentle and ...
35   VISITORS: *(Together)* Brown!

1   GUIDE: What is your point?

2   VISITOR 2: There are a lot of animals out there that you're not

3   giving people a chance to see because of your obsession with

4   brown bears!

5   GUIDE: Yes, but there are a lot more brown bears than any other

6   animal. And we have seventy-eight of them here at our zoo.

7   VISITOR 3: But it would be nice to have a little variety ...

8   GUIDE: Can we please continue our tour? I have another group

9   coming in another ten minutes! *(VISITORS give up and walk*

10   *out, throwing their hands up — all except VISITOR 5, who stays.)*

11   Wait! We're not finished with our tour! Ohhh! *(Turning to*

12   *VISITOR 5)* Well? What are you still doing here?

13   VISITOR 5: I like bears!

14   GUIDE: *(Sighing heavily)* Over here we have our very rare brown

15   bear with no claws ... *(Fade and exit.)*

16

17

18

19

20

21

22

23

24

25

26

27

28

29

30

31

32

33

34

35

Topical Index

*All sketches are listed in alphabetical order
throughout the book for easy reference.*

Scriptural Index

*All sketches are listed in alphabetical order
throughout the book for easy reference.*

About the Author

Daniel Wray wears a number of hats — among them, teacher, author, and dramatist. He is the Inclusion Facilitator for students with significant support needs at Rampart High School. He also teaches several courses for education paraprofessionals through the University of Colorado at Denver. Previously, he taught creative writing, composition, and journalism at Colorado Springs Christian Schools.

Daniel has written several published plays and short stories and recently contributed to the publication of a software program for students with disabilities.

He has served as the Youth Commission Chair for the Rocky Mountain Mennonite Conference for a number of years. In his local church, Beth-El Mennonite, he has been a youth group leader and the drama coordinator. He is also active with Special Olympics as a coach and coordinator for the High School Unified Sports League in his area.

Dan, his wife, and their three children live in Colorado Springs, Colorado.

Order Form

Meriwether Publishing Ltd.
PO Box 7710
Colorado Springs CO 80933-7710
Phone: 800-937-5297 Fax: 719-594-9916
Website: www.meriwether.com

Please send me the following books:

_____ **Service with a Smile #BK-B225** $15.95
by Daniel Wray
52 humorous sketches for Sunday worship

_____ **More Service with a Smile #BK-B266** $15.95
by Daniel Wray
Another helping of humorous sketches for Sunday worship

_____ **Worship Sketches 2 Perform #BK-B242** $15.95
by Steven James
A collection of scripts for two actors

_____ **More Worship Sketches 2 Perform #BK-B258** $14.95
by Steven James
A collection of scripts for two actors

_____ **Isaac Air Freight: The Works #BK-B215** $16.95
by Dan Rupple and Dave Toole
Sketches from the premier Christian comedy group

_____ **Isaac Air Freight: The Works 2 #BK-B243** $16.95
by Dan Rupple and Dave Toole
More sketches from the premier Christian comedy group

_____ **Sermons Alive! #BK-B132** $14.95
by Paul Neale Lessard
52 dramatic sketches for worship services

These and other fine Meriwether Publishing books are available at
your local bookstore or direct from the publisher. Prices subject to
change without notice. Check our website or call for current prices.

Name: _____ e-mail: _____

Organization name: _____

Address: _____

City: _____ State: _____

Zip: _____ Phone: _____

❑ **Check enclosed**

❑ **Visa / MasterCard / Discover #** _____

Expiration
Signature: _____ *date:* _____
(required for credit card orders)

Colorado residents: Please add 3% sales tax.
Shipping: Include $3.95 for the first book and 75¢ for each additional book ordered.

❑ *Please send me a copy of your complete catalog of books and plays.*